TECHNOLOGY IN TODAY'S SCHOOLS

E D I T E D B Y
CYNTHIA WARGER

ASCD

Association for Supervision and
Curriculum Development

Printed in the United States of America.

Typeset on Xerox™ Ventura Publisher 2.0
Printed by Edwards Brothers
Cover Design by Simeon Montesa

ASCD Stock No. 611-90085
ISBN: 0-87120-169-0
Library of Congress
   Catalog Card No. 90-36344
$16.95   OCLC: 21483343

Technology in Today's Schools

Foreword

*O*ver the last few years, there's been a lot of talk about restructuring and how to improve education. Having worked for 25 years as a teacher and school administrator, and now in the educational technology business, I'm painfully aware of the need for change in the schooling process in America. Were we meeting the educational needs of all children in our schools today, or able to absorb into the labor market those individuals who were unsuccessful as students, technology in education might be unnecessary. But schools today do not meet the educational needs of all students, and the labor market is demanding a work force with ever-increasing skills and abilities.

In addition, we cannot effectively individualize instruction with existing student/teacher ratios. And, unfortunately, the teaching methods and learning environments in schools today are neither bias free nor affirmative of diversity. Though not a panacea, technology needs to be looked into as a major resource for enhancing the teaching/learning process. Technology can provide a multi-sensory, bias-free alternative to traditional instructional approaches. It can easily be controlled for quality and equity of access. And it can afford students privacy and individualization as well as control over their own learning. While school improvements through restructuring require attention to effective models of school organization, proven instructional practices and management strategies, and shared expectations of curriculum content, standards, evaluation, and student outcomes, technology must be recognized for its potential impact. Appropriate uses of computer technology, tool application, instructional and management systems software, distance learning capabilities, laser and video systems software, laser and video disks, and other multimedia technology applications must be considered as we restructure schooling.

As leaders in education, we must understand and effectively apply solutions for improving the schooling process. The contributing authors in this book help light our way by telling us how and when to make effective technology decisions.

Donna Jean Carter
ASCD President, 1990-91

Introduction

Cynthia Warger

*T*he last decade of the 20th century is upon us, and with it comes a growing number of reports and documents projecting what our nation's children will need to know in the 21st century, and discussions detailing what educators have and have not done toward these ends.

At the forefront of many of these discussions is technology and how education has fared in integrating technology into the curriculum. As Gibbon (1987) pointed out, the electronic technologies that drive the information explosion are increasingly powerful and, thus, should be used in schools, as they are elsewhere, to represent present and new knowledge. If we are to prepare our children for the future, then we must help them become technologically literate.

For some critics, the technology integration process in the schools has been too slow (Ellison 1989). They are quick to point out that while millions of adults use computers every day, our children only begin to learn about computers in school. A recent survey of over 5,000 educators (NSBA 1988) concluded that educators, in general, are only beginning to tap the potential of technology in classrooms.

Why the hesitance by educators? In 1985, an ASCD *Update* headline proclaimed, "Computer Integration in Instruction Is Stuck." The article went on to characterize educators who were once enthusiastic about technology as now cautious, reflective, and skeptical (Dronka 1988). Educators will point out that many technological developments hit the educational market with razzle-dazzle fanfare and significant price tags, only to have the latest model labeled as obsolete months later. They also point to years of technology experts promising too much and delivering too little. Technological developments, ranging from microcomputers to distance learning satellites to compact discs and video, have each been heralded as a major breakthrough with the potential for revolutionizing education (Ely and Plomp 1988), and each has fallen short of its promise. As recent studies reveal (Becker 1987, Roblyer 1988), evidence of effectiveness is scanty; and existing studies provide little guidance for educators as they decide how to use technology in instruction.

A Practitioner's Approach to Integrating Technology

Much of the early literature on integrating technology in classrooms reflected an unrealistic view of the classroom. It reflected a vision of education not shared by the average practitioner, who viewed teaching and learning as a human-interaction endeavor. We can draw the analogy between the introduction of technology to the classroom and the introduction of the microwave oven. When first introduced, the microwave promised to revolutionize cooking by having the cook merely wrap food in plastic and heat it up. For those of us who took great pride in our cooking, the idea just didn't fly: how could one prepare creamy sauces, saute and brown succulent meats, and bake to perfection rich, luscious desserts in one of those boxes? This changed the very essence of the art that many of us had studied and perfected over years. But, as we've grown to discover the capabilities of microwave cooking, we've come to accept that, although they are wonderful for certain cooking tasks, they cannot replace stove and regular oven cooking altogether. However, when integrated into a cook's normal routine, the microwave is a significant tool for creating a successful meal.

Likewise, technology can be a significant tool in the classroom. Most school systems have made considerable strides in purchasing equipment, preparing teachers, and implementing programs, yet more can be done (Collis 1988). In doing more, however, we should get rid of unrealistic notions that technology can "do it all." Technology is not a panacea for educational problems. The challenge confronting education is not to produce more electronic technology, but rather, to creatively develop the educational potential that the new technologies already offer (Ofiesh 1986). Technology can be used to support education, not supplant it.

Previously, the features promoted in the various educational technologies were not connected to any real problem or issue. The idea of using technology just because it was there evoked imagery of the old microwave commercials of the housewife, who, only knowing how to cook popcorn in the new microwave, prepared a family meal of popcorn fixed six different ways. Using technology for the sake of using technology became much debated. While our heroine in the microwave commercial finds a fine use of the technology in a glowing microwave production of Duck a L'Orange, no corresponding educational coup de grace awaited the user of educational technology. On reflection, some of the less successful uses of educational technology have been observed to occur when it was offered as a solution to a problem that had not been clearly defined (Ely and Plomp 1988).

Perhaps the true test of the new educational technology has been its staying power in schools. Much of this staying power has come from practitioners' finding ways to use the new technologies as "tools" that support the teaching-learning process. The notion of conceptualizing technology as tools, and the impact of doing so, was discussed by Gilbert Valdez (1986):

> Although it is less easy to document, 1985-86 may also become known as the year in which extreme claims — technology totally replacing teachers, on the one hand, or being just another fad, on the other — have been replaced by a more balanced understanding of what technology can and can not do. This year may also mark the departure from overemphasis on programming in favor of broad-based use of technology in many subject areas to enhance teaching and learning.

Many technological solutions are available today, but their success still depends on classroom teachers and how they use the technologies to solve real classroom problems (Barbour 1989). Many of the more popular technology applications in classrooms today do not require substantial changes in the ways teachers teach and provide practical solutions to real teaching dilemmas. There is no single "best use" of technology in schools to improve learning; thus, continued experimentation and sharing of experiential information is encouraged (Office of Technology Assessment 1988). A realistic assessment of the role of technology in education can come only with a deep understanding of how to match its potential power with the needs of learners (Taylor and Cunniff 1988).

Organization of this Book

This book* describes approaches that practitioners and experts working with practitioners have found successful in using technology as a tool to improve learning. How schools choose to use technology depends in part on the vision of the schools' leaders. Knowing how other leaders (defined here as those professionals who make instructional decisions) have confronted issues in

---

*With the exception of the nine school district descriptions and the chapters by Withrow, Mojkowski, Sales and Damyanovich, Valdez and Sollie, Pogrow, and Bowman, the articles were first printed in *To Support the Learner: A Collection of Essays on the Applications of Technology in Education. Enhancing Learning Through Technology*. (Washington, D.C.: Research Applications Division, Office of Educational Research and Improvement (ED), 1989).

using technology as a solution to educational problems can assist us in expanding technology options in our own settings.

The first four chapters of this book deal with general issues in integrating technology into school programs. The next five chapters describe instructional approaches using such technologies as interactive videos, computer-assisted instruction, on-line databases, and telecommunications. Keyboarding is discussed as a necessary skill underlying many instructional approaches. Examples of instruction using technology in the various curriculum areas of science, language arts, humanities, and math are then presented. The needs of special groups are then discussed in chapters on at-risk youth, early childhood education, and ensuring equity for female students. Each chapter offers the reader an example of what might be possible. The remainder of the book is devoted to descriptions of nine districts that have integrated technology into educational programs.

Emerging from the examples in this book is a picture of committed educators who have found realistic and practical ways to integrate technology into their programs. From their work, we gain a true sense of what is now possible in our classrooms.

References

Barbour, A. (1989). "Teachers: The Real Key to Solving Curriculum Problems." *Electronic Learning* 5-8.

Becker, H.J. (1987). "The Impact of Computer Use in Children's Learning: What Research Has Shown and What It Has Not." Report No. 18. Baltimore, Md.: Center for Research on Elementary and Middle Schools, The Johns Hopkins University.

Collis, B. (1988). *Computers, Curriculum, and Whole Class Instruction: Issues and Ideas.* Bellmont, Calif.: Wadsworth Publishing Company.

Dronka, P. (1985). "Computer Integration into Instruction Is Stuck: Experts Blame Unclear Optimal Uses and Three Implementation Problems." *ASCD Update* 27, 5: 1-8.

Ellison, C. (January 1989). "PCs in the Schools: An American Tragedy." *PC/Computing* 96-104.

Ely, D.P., and T. Plomp. (1989). "The Promises of Educational Technology." in *Educational Media and Technology Yearbook 1988*, edited by D.P. Ely. Englewood, Colo.: Libraries Unlimited, Inc., 5-18.

Gibbon, S.Y. (1987). "Learning and Instruction in the Information Age." In *What Curriculum for the Information Age?*, edited by M.A. White. Hillsdale, N.J.: Lawrence Erlbaum Associates, 1-23.

National School Boards Association. (1988). "Thinking about Technology in the Schools: A 1988 Snapshot." Alexandria, Va.: NSBA.

Office of Technology Assessment. (1988). *Power On! New Tools for Teaching and Learning*. OTA-SET-379. Washington, D.C.: Microsoft Press, 299-319.

Roblyer, M.D. (1988). "The Effectiveness of Microcomputers in Education: A Review of the Research for 1980-1987." *T.H.E. Journal* 16, 2: 85-89.

Taylor, R.P., and N. Cunniff. (1988). "Moving Computers and Education Beyond Rhetoric." In *Computing and Education: The Second Frontier*, edited by R.O. McClintock. New York: Teachers College Press.

Valdez, G. (1986). "Realizing the Potential of Educational Technology." *Educational Leadership* 43, 6: 4-6.

1

Where Do We Go Now That the Power's On?

Frank B. Withrow

*I*n the 1980s, we saw a remarkable change in the educational technology resources available to students and teachers. The Office of Technology Assessment (1988) estimated in *Power On*, their study on technology applications in education, that in the United States there are 10,000 pieces of software available for elementary and secondary education and that there is an installed base of 1 computer for every 30 students. In a little more than a decade, some 2 million microcomputers have made their way into classrooms! We also know that instructional television has become a more readily available educational resource. More than 90 percent of the classrooms in the United States have access to video cassette recorders. Distance learning through satellite, fiber optics, and cable television is also available on a daily basis to thousands of students. In fact, a major federal program, Star Schools, is supporting distance learning programs for science, mathematics, and foreign languages in more than 1,000 sites in 40 states.

Now that the power is "on," what can educators expect from technology in the decade ahead? To answer this question, I refer to the recommendations posed in *Power On*. First, there is still a need for more educational technology hardware. Second, teachers need more professional development in the integration of technology into the learning and teaching processes. Third, there needs to be a greater partnership among all groups in the development of the software.

Need for More Technology

If we think of information and communication advances throughout history, we can understand the importance of the new technological tools that are offered to us today. The first and most powerful communication tool was the development of spoken language, which enabled a person to share ideas and experiences with others. With the advent of the written symbol, people became able to share information over time and space. Within the last century, we have taken a quantum leap forward in real-time distance communication. We have developed two systems: one, a person to person telephonic system; the other, a mass broadcast system. Both permeate our lives in a modern, information-rich society.

While the computer is the newest tool in the system, we should not think of it in isolation. The computer brings all forms of communication together into one continuous ribbon of information that can be accessed by the user. As we move into the 1990s, there will be Integrated Service Digital Networks (ISDNs). ISDNs are the fiber optic systems being developed by telephone companies that allow for storage and retrieval of almost unlimited information. Through ISDNs in homes, schools, and businesses, vast databases of information can be accessed. For example, it might be possible in such a system to be watching a television talk show and freeze the picture, touch the speaker on the screen, which would access an article from the speaker's bibliography, leave a message for the speaker, and perhaps even arrange a telephone call with the speaker. Conversely, one might be reading text material, for example, *Hamlet*, and decide to see it performed. From the ISDN database, one might even be able to choose from several different casts. Technically, these things are possible.

There are important issues for educators to consider as the technology matures and becomes more effective. First, schools must develop more capacity to use such systems as they develop. They must also understand that most technology will become obsolete before it wears out. Thus, questions about financing hardware and deciding what to do with hardware that was purchased ten, or even five, years ago must be seen in light of the greater context.

Need for Professional Development

Staff development must be a lifelong experience for teachers who use technology. Teachers must be shown what tools are available and then provided with practical assistance in how to best use those tools in their classrooms. We need to explore new ways that teachers can integrate the technology into the daily lessons of learners.

Obviously, technology can be both a tool and a content resource. A prerecorded television program or software package represents a content resource that can be used by students and teachers. The challenge for teachers is to use these technologies to make the learning process come alive. Using technology as a tool gives the student and teacher new ways to express what they have learned. For example, the computer used as a word processor, desktop publisher, or spreadsheet is a tool for learning. Likewise, an audiotape recorder or video camcorder can serve as a tool for helping students express their ideas.

The content storage capacity of the new technology system can also serve as a powerful information resource. The actual newsreels of political events, such as the audio recordings and video clips of Martin Luther King Jr.'s "I Have a Dream" speech, are resource documents that can bring a new understanding of history to the learner. Also, reference materials stored in videodiscs in the area of bioscience, coupled with computer-controlled indexes, provide valuable experiences for students.

Need to Develop Partnerships

The key to making technology a vital component in education lies in how the resources are gathered together, indexed, and made available to schools in a cost-effective manner. Schools, publishers, and technologists must work together to organize and bring these resources to the learning environment. In one sense, we are already seeing these systems becoming a reality in schools with integrated learning systems. Such systems offer a large library of courseware, management systems, and, to some extent, diagnostic systems to help the teacher and learner navigate through the materials. In tomorrow's world we will have many of the resources of the Library of Congress or something comparable readily available to students. Educators must begin thinking about how to organize and develop such resources so that they can be most effectively used. For example, the thousands of hours of *Sesame Street* that have been produced and developed to work on early reading skills are now provided to us in a linear fashion that is determined by a broadcast schedule. In the future, digital technology can make all of those elements of *Sesame Street* available to the learner on demand.

The capacity of technology to store and retrieve information is massive. The CD-ROM can store some 300,000 pages of text, which equals one thousand 300-page books. Traditional filmstrips with 100 frames can be transferred to videodiscs. On just one side of a disc, we can store 54,000 frames or 540 film-strips, which could encompass entire school libraries.

One of the many barriers to developing technology to its potential for educational purposes is cost. Unfortunately, the market is limited by preconceived notions of price. This raises the question of what is a fair price for intellectual property. On this question, it is critical that schools take the lead in establishing partnerships that will result in creative answers.

*   *   *

To a certain extent, educational technology is always introduced into the schools by outside forces. Technology was primarily developed for entertainment, business, and military purposes. Technology, in and of itself, is not an exemplary teacher. Like a good book, it may inspire students and open new horizons for them. It may stimulate the learner to wonder anew at the world. It may provide a tool to express what one has learned. But in the end, true learning results from interactions among the learner, other learners, and teachers. Technology, for all of its promise, cannot substitute for the basic rules of a good learning environment.

References

Office of Technology Assessment. (1988). *Power On! New Tools for Teaching and Learning.* GPO 052-003-01125. Washington, D.C.: U.S. Government Printing Office.

Office of Technology Assessment. (1989). *Linking for Learning: A New Course for Education.* GPO 052-003-01170-1. Washington, D.C.: U.S. Government Printing Office.

2

A Curriculum for the Information Age

Mary Alice White

*E*ach social institution and work setting relies on particular information processes that are central to its operations. Financial institutions rely on the speed of processing market information; medicine relies on the analysis of data to arrive at a diagnosis and treatment plan; science relies on the collection of multiple observations to establish meaningful patterns; and journalism relies on the speed of access to a newsworthy event and the speed of its communication to an audience.

Education too, relies on students' being able to acquire information, analyze it, and communicate their learnings. However, the way education uses information technologies differs from the way other professions use the same technologies. As we move into the next decade, knowledge of how other professions use technologies should be used to expand how educators use the technologies to improve learning and teaching.

Institutional Processes Changed by the Technologies

Several work processes have been significantly enhanced by technology. A description of each follows.

Planning. Planning is a critical process in many settings, whether it is financial, strategic, operational, logistical, or political. The process of planning is carried out differently in banks, investment houses, the military, federal and state governments, corporations, small businesses,and universities. Planning has been radically altered by the introduction of computers and spreadsheet software. It is now possible to actually see in numeric form the impact that specific change in one variable will make on a host of others, projected into the future.

Information Access. Members of the financial community rely on the quickness of information retrieval to make their decisions, as we saw so vividly in the October 1987 stock market decline. Obviously, up-to-the-minute worldwide financial databases offer traders an enormous advantage. In fact, there is some concern about whether such instantaneous information should in some way be controlled because of its ability to cause a wave of institutional buying or selling on Wall Street and other world markets. The media depend on the speed of transmission to receive and broadcast the news. Politicians are anxious to be seen and heard on the media as quickly as possible after a newsworthy event. Instant information is the currency of electronic media.

Electronic databases have also transformed the extent to which we can access information. In law, for instance, a database makes it possible for lawyers to search for previous decisions in a few minutes by typing in key phrases of the legal points of interest. In medicine, a physician can type in a patient's symptoms and receive possible diagnoses within seconds from a database that incorporates medical knowledge and experience far beyond that of the user. Reporters and writers can search a database of newspapers and magazines to find, instantaneously, the background of a certain person or subject.

Tapping into a database would not be practical if it were not convenient. The availability of computers and modems means that information can be brought up on the screen quickly and easily (although some databases are still unnecessarily difficult to navigate). Instead of traveling to the appropriate library to search for the relevant books, a scholar can call up an exhaustive list of references on a monitor in a few minutes and decide which are worth pursuing.

Information Management. Among the needs of many institutions and work settings are the processes of storing information, analyzing what is stored, and representing that information in meaningful ways. These information processes are central to any setting that must work with large amounts of data. In agriculture, there is a need to store large amounts of information about the condition of crops around the world; businesses must store information about their customers and their suppliers; the federal government cannot survive without storing huge amounts of information about taxpayers; and scientific research requires large pools of recorded information.

In all of these settings, computers have transformed the process of storing information, from larger computer systems to many small microcomputers connected to mass storage devices. The new laser systems for storage, including the CD-ROM, are providing a cost-effective, massive storage system for all types of computers.

Information that is stored needs to be processed. Large amounts of data are now analyzed by computerized statistical methods to show trends and differences between groups of data. Information analysis can also compare information from several databases so that, for example, an individual's credit standing can be compared to a record of purchases, phone calls, passport visas, and voter registration. While this represents a resource for some, it also raises major issues of privacy, which as a society we must resolve.

Because computers have made the storage and analysis of mass data possible, more numeric information has been made available than the human mind can comprehend easily. One answer to this problem has been the development of graphic and pictorial (iconic) displays of data. These represent a large amount of numeric information in graphic form, in pictures of trends, in three-dimensional figures for engineers and architects, and in visual displays of observations that produce meaningful patterns to the informed eye. It is ironic that the computer's ability to produce masses of numerical information has resulted in the use of imagery to help humans understand what the computer can produce. The great number cruncher now needs an image maker.

Communication. Just as information itself has changed, so has access to it, storage and analysis of it, and its representation. We are also finding that the nature of communication is changing with the new information technologies. Many journalists have found that the word processor is a better writing tool than a typewriter or a pencil because it is easier, faster, more flexible, and able to produce perfect copy for almost anyone. Salespersons and business executives find that portable computers give them writing power and constant communication with a home office.

Software programs allow authors to add graphics easily into business reports, presentations, letters, and newsletters. Desktop publishing can put the power of the printing press into the hands of any individual. Software programs now lay out pages, allow one to insert graphics and pictures, and change type styles—in fact, do virtually anything that a printing house would do.

Communication from one computer user to another is also available, either through a local network or one of the many commercial or scientific networks now in operation. Through a modem and a phone line, a computer owner can communicate with any other similar owner, almost anywhere in the world. We are also seeing increased teleconferencing, both audio and video, as

7

well as facsimile use, with teleconferencing becoming more feasible for every-day transmissions.

The burgeoning world of pictorial communications via television, film, and videotape is being transformed by the availability of videotape players, video cameras, and new electronic cameras that display still photographs through our television screens. By the mid-1990s, digitized home television sets will have the potential to become the center for home communications systems. They will provide us with the images and sounds of television, still images, screens of text, stereo sound, and telephonic services, all controlled by our computers. Such hypermedia systems are already available in prototypical research formats. The digital design will increase the ease of manufacturing and the capacity and power of the systems, and reduce cost. Within our home communication systems all of the pictorial processes of the home entertainment industry, and graphic, text, and statistical resources of the business world, will be available.

How we communicate is changing rather quickly. Communication is becoming faster; it can reach more people, and do so in print formats, numeric and graphic form, or images.

Creative Expression. Graphic artists have found tools of enormous power that make animation a simpler process and give the artist power to create, on screen, a range of visual effects that would have been too time consuming to create by hand. Musicians use music synthesizers, which can imitate the sound of any instrument in any combination, to write music more quickly and easily. The more sophisticated of these music synthesizers have even found their way to the stage of Carnegie Hall.

The significance of the change in communication technology is not just that the work is being done differently, but that the processes involved in the work are changing. People now have to think differently about how they do their work. The mental operations involved are changing as information becomes more accessible, faster, and of greater magnitude. How we think about a problem changes when we can view the problem through imagery.

Educational Processes Changed by the Technologies

How are these technologies changing the field of education? Public schools have installed computers, bought software, trained teachers to use computers, installed computer laboratories, and initiated classes in computer programming. Some have even bought video disc equipment, video cameras, and modems and have joined networks.

Yet there is a difference between what is happening in education and what is happening in other work settings. The difference is that while other institutions and work settings have adopted the technologies into the heart of their functioning, and the technologies, in turn, have changed the nature of work, *education has not changed a single basic process that is essential to its operation.* Education has tended to keep the technologies apart from the basic processes of learning and teaching. Software is used in schools largely for drill and practice, for peripheral work for the gifted, or for remedial work for the slower students. The continuing work of mainstream education has remained largely unaffected.

It is true that schools have lacked sufficient money to invest in technologies. But a more basic problem is that educators have not seen that the information technologies are just as central to the operations of education as they are to business, research, and the arts. Without this understanding, there can be no conceptual framework for the role of technologies in education. Without the conceptual framework, there has been no commitment to invest in the technologies as a rational educational investment.

The basic processes of education include acquiring information, developing communication and cognitive skills, and encouraging certain attitudes and behaviors in students. The information technologies are superb at information access, analysis, and organization. They have large communication capacities and considerable potential for helping learners acquire certain cognitive skills. Yet, the technologies are inserted around the edges of the curriculum, with students typically assigned only 20-40 minutes a week to a computer laboratory. The rest of the curriculum stays the same.

A Curriculum for the Information Age

What is the answer for education? Let us recall how other institutions and work settings have used these technologies to see what might be learned.

The point is not that schools should imitate the workplace in their uses of technology. But because many institutions and work settings have found their basic operation transformed through the use of technology, it makes sense for schools to ask how they can transform their environment as well. Do these technologies offer any learning or teaching value for the basic processes of acquiring information and certain communication and cognitive skills?

These technologies can change the nature of information itself and how we represent it. They can change how we view information cognitively. These are "learning technologies."

How might education adapt these technologies into a curriculum for the information age?

Planning. At the appropriate age, perhaps as early as the fifth or sixth grade, students could be learning how to use planning as a cognitive skill in combination with spreadsheet types of software. Students do not need to be taught how to project a business plan or a profit-and-loss statement, but they could project demographic changes in their city or village and plan how to deal with the anticipated results. When learning the history of their state and town, they could also learn about its projected future. Students might also complete a project on occupational supply and demand, which might influence their career choices. Or they could learn to plan their own expenditures, and see — literally — the impact of a change in one variable on their total budget.

Information Access. Students need to know how to access information through technologies, but they also need to learn how to do so with some judgment. The speed of transmission creates an illusion that the most recent is the best, or most important, or most accurate, which is not necessarily true. A second problem is that only recent information is typically available in data banks, although this will change in time. If students access information at present, they will receive an inflated view of the past few years, and run the risk of developing a distorted historical perspective.

Databases are useful tools to students, which they need to know how to search--a fairly complex cognitive process. It requires both a conceptual schema around which information can be organized and at least some grasp of the scope of the information that may be available. If well taught, the schema should be linked to how the database is categorized: to its "search terms" or "key words." This activity would be appropriate for late elementary or junior high school students.

Knowing how to access information from a variety of databases means that students could learn how to use a wide range of reference materials, including computer databases, CD-ROM discs, and videodiscs. Knowing how to use reference sources is the beginning of learning how to check the accuracy of information and how to discover what one does not know, both of which encourage learning on one's own.

Information Management. Learning how to store information, analyze it, and represent it to others are basic skills for the information age, as well as basic educational skills. Students need not create and store in memory vast quantities of information, as do research scientists, but they do need to know how to store information relevant to their own education.

In the near future, students may use their own computers to store school-relevant information. Until then, it would be useful for them to learn the skills for storing information so that it is easily retrievable. Learning this skill is likely to increase the amount of information stored and to increase its utilization, both extremely useful skills.

The analysis of information is another essential skill, both for the workplace and for education. Students could learn how to use statistical software to analyze information from social studies, science, or mathematics, and in turn, develop an appreciation of how to treat mass data and how to make meaningful comparisons.

The representation of data is a new skill, becoming more important as the human mind tries to comprehend thousands of pieces of data. The representation of numerical information in iconic form is an important new communication skill; students should learn how to communicate information iconically, graphically, and with mapping techniques. Software is available that makes such tasks feasible, but schools need to go beyond these information management skills to allow students to deal with information itself—what it is, how it is changing, and how to evaluate it.

Communication. One of the major tasks of education is to teach communication skills. A powerful tool for written communication is a word processor, which has been demonstrated to improve the speed and ease with which students revise and publish their work. If writing as practiced in the information age is to be taken seriously, many more word processors are needed in the classrooms where the children are, not off in laboratories.

When we turn to pictorial techniques of communication, we step into the world of imagery. Imagery dominates all of entertainment, delivers the news, carries political messages to voters, advertises what to purchase, sets fashions, transmits values through modeling of behavior, portrays occupations to young viewers, accentuates the glory of sports and entertainment figures, implies what is appropriate sexual behavior, and depicts family and home life. Education for the information age takes on a special role in teaching students how to "read" images, a skill integral to creative expression.

Creative Expression. Music is certainly being made easier to learn. Notation can be learned more easily with technology, and composing and music editing are easier as well. In the field of graphic arts, reasonably priced software now makes page layout possible. Graphic databases are numerous; creating graphic designs and art has become a serious undertaking. Each could appropriately fit into the curriculum.

*　*　*

11

These then are five work processes that have been radically altered through the technologies: planning, information access, information management, communication, and creative expression. These changes mean that people are thinking differently about how they carry out their work and how they imagine it. The questions I am raising here are: When will educators think differently about their work? When will educators use these technologies to rethink the curriculums?

3

Developing Technology Applications for Transforming Curriculum and Instruction

Charles Mojkowski

*T*he integration of computers and other technologies into curriculum and instructional practices continues to serve as the "Holy Grail" for educational technology advocates. Despite the increase in the numbers of computers and the enthusiastic reports in the technology journals, their potential to improve learning experiences for students remains largely unrealized.

The questions that teachers, administrators, and researchers have asked for several years remain:

1. How should existing curriculums and pedagogy be redesigned to accommodate and maximize the use of the technology?

2. What are the most appropriate ways to bring technology into the curriculum?

3. How can computers and other new technological tools be used as catalysts to revitalize existing curriculums and instruction within and across subject areas?

That these questions persist is testimony to the inadequate quantity and quality of documentation and information regarding the effectiveness of technology in the classroom (Becker 1987, Bracey 1989). What follows is a description of what we know about these questions.

Background of These Issues

Despite the growing number of computers and other new technology tools in schools, several research reports indicate that their actual use is neither extensive nor appropriate. Pogrow, in assessing the current status, argues:

> In general, (a) advocacy around the new technology agendas, (b) a desire to disseminate the technology as widely as possible, and (c) naivete about the complexity of processes needed to enhance learning have all conspired to produce patterns of computer use that make it almost impossible for computers to contribute to the improvement of learning. . . . The reality is that there is little evidence that current approaches to using computers enhance learning in measurable ways. (Pogrow 1988)

What is often not made clear is that although computer technologies can support a revitalized curriculum and pedagogy, they may have a more limited role in actually catalyzing or initiating the changes. Unless educators are willing to reconceptualize curriculum and instruction (and perhaps the organization and process of schooling itself), they will probably need to be quite patient in expecting transformation to occur through the use of computers and other tools.

In fact, ample evidence shows that computers, videodiscs, CD-ROM, and telecommunications can be integrated into the schools without **appreciably** altering or improving curriculum and instruction. Indeed, experts have argued that the majority of technology applications in elementary and secondary schools are automating and perpetuating learning outcomes and teaching-learning practices that are themselves in desperate need of reform (Nix 1988, Pea and Soloway 1987, Perkins and Salomon 1989).

How Technology Is Being Used

Despite the sparse but robust claims that technology tools can contribute to a revitalized curriculum, replication of exemplary practices is meager. Instead, the computers are predominantly used as instructional devices, usually for computer-assisted instruction (CAI), that deal primarily with low-level skills. Unfortunately, this type of pedagogical approach contrasts sharply with recommendations by those seeking curriculum transformation (Laboratory of Comparative Human Cognition 1989, Schwartz 1989, Weir 1989).

In fact, researchers (Wiske and Zodhiates 1988) report that the traditional use of CAI as an instructional technique has little impact on teachers' use of other instructional strategies (e.g., organization of content, organization of students, teaching repertoires, use of materials and equipment, and student performance assessment). Whether or not the CAI accomplishes mastery more effectively and efficiently, teachers using CAI tend not to focus on more complex language-processing and problem-solving skills.

Impediments to Integration

Curriculum-Instruction-Technology Mismatch

Just what is it that Pogrow (1988) is referring to when he cites the "patterns of computer use that make it almost impossible for computers to contribute to the improvement of learning"? The most prominent pattern is the substantial dissonance that exists between the rhetoric of curriculum and instructional reform and the ways teachers and administrators use technology. The reform messages speak of the thinking child, the independent and self-motivated learner who is able to communicate effectively and work cooperatively on real-world learning tasks. Juxtaposed to this image of transformed schooling are the predominant uses of computers as CAI devices.

Some researchers have also questioned the equity of the use of low-level CAI for disadvantaged and other special-needs children, while creative tool applications are employed with more able students (Laboratory of Comparative Human Cognition 1989). Such an approach is based on a remedial and deficit-oriented pedagogy that may be inadequate and perhaps even detrimental to the needs of these children (Brandt 1986, Levin 1987). As long as these low-level uses of computers predominate, it will be difficult to move technology into a catalytic position.

Technology on the Periphery of School Improvement

In many districts and schools, technology applications, even in their most exemplary forms, exist primarily at the periphery of the organization, unconnected to the district's improvement activities. This circumstance is largely attributable to the way that technology has developed in schools: in a grassroots, primarily entrepreneurial pattern.

This entrepreneurial pattern has advantages and disadvantages. An advantage is that teachers are freed to create innovative technology applications. A disadvantage is that these entrepreneurial ways often do not serve the priority improvement goals in the district or school. Moreover, these entrepreneurial initiatives are difficult to disseminate and replicate to other teachers who are less motivated, less knowledgeable, or less entrepreneurial in their disposition to change.

Often, the persons who manage the technology program are entrepreneurs themselves, and flourish in an isolated, organizational corner of the district or school. In the absence of well-articulated district and school improvement plans, technology initiatives often go their own way, unconnected to district and school improvement priorities. Even where these applications are exemplary, their separation from those priorities makes their justification, particularly their cost-benefit appraisal, problematic. When this separation is combined with the inadequate quantity and quality of documentation and evaluation information, these applications become tenuous at best.

Lack of a Strategic Framework

The absence of districtwide plans for technology applications has been cited as unacceptable by such divergent sources as the National Governors Association (1986), the National School Boards Association (Perelman 1987), and the U.S. Office of Technology Assessment (1988). It is not uncommon for a district to spend hundreds of thousands of dollars on computers and other components of a technology support system without a *curriculum-based plan* for their use.

The plans that do exist often are based on faulty and piecemeal strategies and tactics. Further, some of these plans do not define a strategy for bringing about the transformation of curriculum and instruction using technology as both a catalyst and support. Without such a strategic approach, technology applications, even whole "technology curriculums," have been developed on the periphery of mainstream school and curriculum improvement. When this occurs, there is the risk that the technology curriculums will be unrelated to the content area curriculums that they purport to serve.

How Might These Impediments Be Addressed?

None of these impediments is insurmountable. Indeed, for each, exemplary approaches are operating in lighthouse schools and districts around the country. Five actions appear to characterize these exemplary efforts.

Curriculum First, Technology Second

Districts that use technology appropriately and effectively spend time working on curriculum revitalization. They work toward a better understanding among their staff of the vision of schooling they want. They decide not only what outcomes they want for children, but how they wish teachers and students to accomplish those outcomes. They give increased attention to thinking, problem-solving, and learning-to-learn skills within and across the disciplines.

Technology Linked to District and School Improvement Priorities

Exemplary districts link technology to school improvement priorities. They focus their limited technology resources on designing and implementing a technology support system that addresses the priorities established by the community and district, and not on bringing in the latest and best technology.

Developing a Strategic Sense

Successful districts develop a technology support system plan that is guided by its own vision, mission, and goals. These statements are linked to those that guide the district and schools in their improvement processes. The technology support system plan addresses not only the district's priority outcomes (e.g., improving thinking and learning-to-learn skills), but the teaching and learning environments that the district wants to establish. These districts understand the change process and incorporate these understandings into their plans.

Simultaneous Transformation and Integration

Given the need to work incrementally and simultaneously on both fronts—curriculum transformation and technology integration—some districts use a commonly accepted instructional planning tool: the unit plan. By building on a task and a product familiar to most teachers, these districts are able to extend the typical conceptualization of instructional units. These include attention to technology applications with a special emphasis on tool applications that extend and support incremental transformations in teaching and learning, and are based on an improving knowledge base in the education sciences.

The unit plan is a device for supporting integrative teaching, for blending the specific knowledge, skills, and attitudes of a discipline with the more generic skills (thinking/reasoning, learning/study, information acquisition and use, and problem solving) that need to be developed across several disciplines. The instructional unit plan is a

- design for teaching a unified segment or component of the curriculum;
- "bridge" that links daily instruction to the district's curriculum framework;
- road map for preparing daily lessons;
- means of accomplishing integrated teaching of skills and information;
- mechanism for sharing instructional plans among faculty;
- means of incorporating changes in instructional strategies; and
- means for integrating technology tool applications.

The process of developing unit plans provides an ideal forum for staff development and a practical context in which questions about transformations in teaching and learning practices can be addressed. Within this context, it is easier to select technology applications that move beyond simplistic drill-and-practice and tutorial software.

Incorporating appropriate technology applications into instructional units is not a casual process, however. The technology resource specialists must be deliberate in their identification of opportunities for technology integration. This process of instructional unit development avoids a common syndrome observed in many districts: curriculum improvement committees working independently from technology resource specialists (Mojkowski 1987).

Documentation and Evaluation

If students in an information-rich environment must learn how to evaluate the quality and usefulness of information, make decisions and solve problems with it, and communicate their new knowledge to others, then assessments need to monitor progress in mastering these competencies using appropriate technology tools.

Exemplary districts maintain documentation and evaluation processes for the use of their technology support services. They monitor the implementation of technology applications, track student performance in mastering technology applications competencies, and assess the effectiveness of technology support systems in contributing to the accomplishment of district and school improvement priorities.

*   *   *

Strategic and programmatic approaches to applying technology to the curriculum are designed to obtain the maximum contribution from computers to the revitalization of teaching and learning. Without a reconceptualization of learning outcomes, and the way the teaching and learning process is organized and managed, the predominant applications of technology are likely to continue to serve only an archaic, automated function.

Using computers and other technologies as levers to transform schooling is likely to produce meager, short-term results. Any large-scale transformation of the ways that technology is used is linked to the manner, form, and pace of the existing system. Therefore, districts might do better to work on transformation and integration simultaneously, in a dialectic fashion, using small advances in one area as catalysts for supporting small advances in another.

What is less clear is what strategy will move us from the existing largely entrepreneurial system of advanced technology users to a situation in which all teachers are required to use certain technology tools as part of the curriculum. If the research is correct—and the meta-learning accomplished through technology is important—then we must help teachers operate on that knowledge. Some of these requirements are not amenable to implementation through knowledge acquisition. Very different strategies, ones that move beyond volunteerism, are needed. It is likely that, as Kuhn (1962) suggests, our "normal science" of technology use will not result in any significant transformation until the transformation in teaching and learning takes place.

A strategy for bringing about a transformation of curriculum and instruction with and through a technology support system requires a deliberate and dialectic process in which incremental modifications in curriculum and instruction are matched and supported with technology tool applications that, in turn, stimulate additional transformations in curriculum and instruction. The strategy is a deliberate attempt to bridge the gap between the actual and the potential; between the islands of technology innovation and the perpetual pilot programs conducted by a small core of voracious volunteers and the teachers who often do not use technology at all to support their teaching. Using an incremental approach to the accomplishment of the grand design, classroom teachers and technology resource specialists, through successive approximations, can address the requirements of a transformed curriculum.

References

Archibald, D., and F. Newmann. (1988). *Beyond Standardized Testing*. Reston, Va.: National Association of Secondary School Principals.

Becker, H.J. (1987). *The Impact of Computer Use on Children's Learning: What Research Has Shown and What It Has Not.* Baltimore, Md.: Center for Social Organization of Schools, Johns Hopkins University.

Bracey, G. (1989). "1988-89: The Year of Negative Conclusions—But There's Hope!" *Electronic Learning* 8, 8: 22-24.

Brandt, R.S. (1986). "On Improving Achievement of Minority Children: A Conversation with James Comer." *Educational Leadership* 43, 5: 13-17.

Brandt, R.S. (1988). "Introduction: What Should Schools Teach?" In *Content of the Curriculum* (1988 ASCD Yearbook), edited by R.S. Brandt. Alexandria, Va: Association for Supervision and Curriculum Development.

Crandall, D.P. (1987). "Strategic Planning Issues that Bear on the Success of School Improvement Efforts." *Educational Administration Quarterly* 22, 3: 21-53.

Goldberg, B. (1988). "Restructuring and Technology: Part One." *Radius.* Washington, DC: American Federation of Teachers.

Hord, S., G. Hall, L. Huling-Austin, and W.L. Rutherford. (1987). *Taking Charge of Change.* Alexandria, Va.: Association for Supervision and Curriculum Development.

Kuhn, T. (1970). *The Structure of Scientific Revolutions.* Chicago: The University of Chicago Press.

Laboratory of Comparative Human Cognition. (1989). San Diego: University of California. "Kids and Computers: A Positive Vision of the Future." *Harvard Educational Review* 59, 1: 73-86.

Levin, H.M. (1987). "Accelerated Schools for Disadvantaged Students." *Educational Leadership* 44, 6: 19-21.

Mojkowski, C. (1987). "Technology and Curriculum: Will the Promised Revolution Take Place?" *NASSP Bulletin* 71, 496: 113-118.

Mojkowski, C. (1989). "Transforming Curriculum and Instruction with Technology." A paper presented at Annual American Educational Research Association meeting in San Francisco.

Morton, C., and C. Mojkowski. (1989). "The Dialog Paradigm: A Model for Rethinking Schooling." A paper presented at Annual American Educational Research Association meeting in San Francisco.

National Governors Association. (1986). *Time for Results.* Washington, D.C.: NGA, Center for Policy Research and Analysis.

Nix, D. (1988). "Should Computers Know What You Can Do With Them?" *Teachers College Record.*

Office of Technology Assessment. (1988). *Power On! New Tools for Teaching and Learning.* Washington, D.C.: Government Printing Office.

Pea, R.D., and E. Soloway. (1987). *Mechanisms for Facilitating a Vital and Dynamic Education System: Fundamental Roles for Education, Science and Technology*. Washington, D.C.: Office of Technology Assessment.

Perelman, L.J. (1987). *Technology and the Transformation of Schools*. Washington, D.C.: National School Boards Association.

Perkins, D.N., and G. Salomon. (1989). "Are Cognitive Skills Context-Bound?" *Educational Researcher*. 18, 1: 16-25.

Pogrow, S. (1988). "The Computer Movement Cover-Up." *Electronic Learning* 7, 7: 6-7.

Resnick, L.B., and L.E. Klopfer. (1989). "Toward the Thinking Curriculum: Concluding Remarks." In *Toward the Thinking Curriculum: Current Cognitive Research* (ASCD Yearbook), edited by L.B. Resnick and L.E. Klopfer. Alexandria, Va.: Association for Supervision and Curriculum Development.

Schwartz, J.L. (1989). "Intellectual Mirrors: A Step in the Direction of Making Schools Knowledge-Making Places." *Harvard Educational Review*. 59, 1: 51-61.

Weir, S. (1989). "The Computer in Schools: Machine as Humanizer." *Harvard Educational Review* 59, 1: 61-73.

Wiske, M.S., and P. Zodhiates. (1988). *How Technology Affects Teaching*. Cambridge: Harvard Graduate School of Education, Educational Technology Center, and Education Development Center, Inc.

4

A Model for Making Decisions about Computer and Technology Implementation

Gregory C. Sales
Michael Damyanovich

*M*innesota's Independent School District
(ISD) 279, Osseo Area Schools, is a suburban Minneapolis school district serving several small communities in an area that covers more than 66 square miles. The district's population is growing, with almost 19,000 students currently enrolled in 18 elementary, 3 middle/junior high, and 2 high schools. These schools are staffed by over 1,200 teachers and administrators.

In recent years, ISD 279, like other districts of this size and type, has faced a continuous barrage of opportunities and obligations to explore new applications of instructional technologies. Administrators, teachers, parents, developers, vendors, and others seemed endlessly involved in lobbying or negotiating for the adoption of another innovation. Management of these projects became a serious concern, with limited financial and personnel resources dictating that effective implementation decisions be made. It became clear that a process was needed to help determine which proposed innovations could be meaningfully implemented with such finite resources.

For ISD 279, a Computer/Technology Advisory Committee, made up of teachers, administrators, parents, and a university representative, has proved to be the answer. And for nearly four years, ISD 279 has used this unique process to assist with decision making about the implementation of new technologies and/or technology-related teaching strategies into the curriculum. The process is based on practical experience and research on the implementation of education innovations (Fullan 1982; Hall, George, and Rutherford 1979; Showers, Joyce, and Bennett 1987; Stasz and Shavelson 1985).

Chaired by a former classroom teacher, and working from within the District Education Service Center, the Advisory Committee has five responsibilities:

1. To establish local investigations involving computers and related technology.

2. To receive reports from investigation sites.

3. To evaluate local investigations and studies at external sites.

4. To communicate outcomes of investigations to standing committees or task forces.

5. To make recommendations for districtwide installation of effective computer/technology applications to the Directors of Instructional Support Services, Elementary Education, and Secondary Education.

Providing opportunities to investigate as many promising educational innovations as possible is central to fulfillment of the Advisory Committee's mission. Therefore, a systematic strategy involving six steps has been developed. Each step is listed here and is elaborated upon more fully in the following paragraphs.

1. Elicit proposals from teachers and building-level administrators interested in investigating a specific application on a small scale.

2. Review proposals and determine which are to be funded.

3. Provide support for funded investigations to assure design, implementation, and evaluation.

4. Assign committee members to visit investigation sites to observe the implementation.

5. Require personnel involved in the investigation to file and present a formal report to the committee.

6. As a committee, recommend whether an investigation should be terminated, continued in order to gather more data, or implemented districtwide.

Eliciting Proposals. In the fall of each year, a newsletter is distributed throughout the district announcing the investigations funded for the upcoming year and recognizing the individuals and schools involved (see Figure 4.1 for a partial listing of previous investigations). This newsletter serves to stimulate or rekindle interest in the investigation process. During winter quarter, a call for proposals is made and all teachers and administrators, including those who may have previously expressed interest, are encouraged to submit formal proposals.

Figure 4.1

A Partial Listing of Investigations Approved by the Advisory Committee

1987-1988

Voyage of the Mimi
Mastery management matched to elementary mathematics
Classroom computer matched to mathematics intervention strategies
Videodisc courseware matched to low-achievement areas of mathematics
Videotape loan library
Two-way television for precocious readers
Graphics capabilities of the Apple IIGS in art
Interactive videodisc authoring — science

1988-1989

Mathematics management (elementary) on the Omninet network
Software loan system for "Assurance of Mastery"
Foreign language instruction with videodiscs
Telecommunication technology in business education (senior high school)
Telecommunication technology in the elementary curriculum
Desktop publishing in the elementary curriculum
Algebra I — networked computer-based instruction and management

---

In light of the busy schedule of those making proposals, and in an effort to elicit as many good proposals as possible, the format for proposing an investigation is short and focused (see Figure 4.2). Background information for the project, the objectives or intent of the investigation, hardware and software needs, the target population, and staff training requirements must be included.

Figure 4.2

An Annotated Investigation Proposal Form for Computer/Technology Investigation Proposal

Name of person submitting proposal_____

Date _____

Building _____

Phone _____

Title of Proposal _____

Background
Briefly describe a *problem* you would try to resolve, or *a goal* you would attempt to achieve, *a new form of technology* you want to try, or a *new application* you want to investigate.

Intent of the Investigation
Briefly describe how this investigation would increase efficiency.
Here are some examples:
1. Use of this technology promotes cost effectiveness (less labor/ increased production)
2. Use of this technology decreases time on task.
3. Use of this technology increases time on task.
4 Use of this technology increases understanding and/or retention of information.
5. Use of this technology decreases attrition (absence-dropouts).
6. Use of this technology facilitates reaching a larger audience.
7. Use of this technology increases attention or interest.

Software/Hardware Requirements
Identify specific hardware and software needed and a budget.

Target Population
Identify the student population that will participate in the investigation.

Staff Training Requirements
Identify the training budget necessary to get the investigation underway.

Proposal Review. In late February or early March, the Advisory Committee meets to review the proposals for new investigations. Proposals usually involve a minimum number of teachers, classrooms, and grade levels.

Criteria for selection include demonstrated need, demonstrated interest among teachers, the number of students to be served if the implementation is successful, potential for cost effectiveness, and degree of innovation. In addition, an attempt is made to see that investigations are not concentrated at a single grade level or within a few schools.

The Advisory Committee forwards recommendations for future investigations to the administrative staff for consideration during budget planning. Final approval of investigations is contingent on allocation of adequate resources.

Support. In addition to securing financial support for materials and training, the Advisory Committee makes recommendations on design, implementation, and evaluation. Technical support is also available from the staff in the district's Education Service Center. Every effort is made to ensure that the implementation and evaluation are as complete as possible so that an accurate assessment of the implementation versus potential can be made.

Visits and Observations. Each member of the Advisory Committee is asked to identify several investigations of particular interest and to serve on observation teams. These teams serve several functions. Aside from the obvious data-gathering functions, they also demonstrate to the teachers involved that the Advisory Committee is interested in the investigation. Their visits provide an opportunity for the teachers to discuss their experiences.

Observers are asked to complete observation forms (see Figure 4.3 for a list of questions) at each site. The forms are used to focus the observer's attention to issues related to operation and management, quality of materials, student attitude and achievement, curriculum and instructional practice, and the investigator's current perceptions of the investigations' progress.

Figure 4.3

Observation Questions
Computer/Technology Investigations

MANAGEMENT/OPERATIONS

1. How was the technology used (large groups, small groups and/or individuals)?
2. Was the technology usable in the classroom and/or laboratory?
3. Did the technology require support staff to operate?
4. Was the technology easy to use?
5. Was the technology obtrusive?
6. Does this system improve teacher decision making? (e.g., reteaching, small grouping, placement)
7. Does this system replace manual clerical work? (e.g., test scoring, progress reporting, and/or recordkeeping)
8. Does the system release teachers from clerical work?
9.. Does the use of the system increase the teachers' clerical work?
10. Is there a ratio of teachers/classroom to the amount of equipment per station? To number of stations per building?
11. What types of prerequisite skills are necessary for effective training (hardware, software, management)?
12. How much training was required with the system?
13. Was proficiency necessary before application or was some on-the-job training justified?
14. What follow-up training should occur?
15. Did the system facilitate activities that could/would not be done otherwise?
16. What will we lose/trade off through application of this system? (teacher time, personal interaction, affective curriculum)
17. Did the system introduce/facilitate or promote student and/or staff behavior appropriate to the "school of the future"? (Questions 15-17 also apply to the other categories.)

QUALITY/APPROPRIATENESS OF MATERIALS

1. Was the hardware reliable under normal use?
2. Was the hardware application specific or flexible?
3. Was the hardware matched to the target group?
4. Was the software compatible with our hardware?
5. Are network versions, lab packs, or site licenses available?
6. Was the software easy to use?
7. Was the software worth the effort (time efficient) for the output obtained?

Continued

8. Was the software of good instructional design? Were there any obvious shortcomings as you worked with it? Any aspects or features you wished it contained?

9. Was the software readily available?

STUDENT ACHIEVEMENT AND ATTITUDE

1. What is the impact of use on student achievement on traditional objectives?

2. Does use promote attainment of new student competencies associated with computers and related technology?

3. Are new student competencies more possible or enhanced by this technology?

4. Were the students willing to use the system at first? Over the long haul?

5. Were the students confused by the system at first? Over the long haul?

6. Did students choose to use the system over other alternatives?

CURRICULUM AND INSTRUCTIONAL PRACTICE

1. Does use aid the learner in attaining currently defined curriculum objectives?

2. Does use suggest modification of current curriculum objectives or addition of a new, describable pool?

3. What principles of instruction are employed through use of the system?

    a. Retention

    b. Motivation

    c. Reinforcement

4. Does the system increase student efficiency in practicing target behaviors? (e.g., does word processing enhance guided and independent practice of specific writing skills?)

5. Is the system used to provide corrective teaching as needed?

6. Does the system allow for adjusting the instructional time (time on task) to enable students to reach outcome goals successfully?

Investigator(s) Report. Individuals involved in each investigation are required to make a formal presentation and to file a brief report to the Advisory Committee upon completion of the investigation. These reports describe the implementation, summarize the results, and present recommendations.

Committee Recommendations. The Advisory Committee makes recommendations to the district's central administration based on the observations and reports filed on each investigation. Possible recommendations are:

- Discontinue — terminate an investigation and consider it unsuccessful or inappropriate.
- Continue — continue an investigation so that additional data can be gathered before a more specific recommendation can be made.
- Extend — extend the scope of an investigation by adding related hardware or software at the original site.
- Expand (Pilot) — add additional sites to determine if the implementation can be generalized.
- Install — implement the innovation (in appropriate classes or at the appropriate level).

The Advisory Committee's recommendations are, of course, advisory only. Decisions, at the district level, are made after considering the recommendation in light of the budget, curriculum plans, reports from other committees, and other relevant information.

Discussion

The benefits, both direct and indirect, of the investigation made possible through the Computer/Technology Advisory Committee process have been many. Perhaps the most important of these is that the district has been able to investigate the potential benefits of a variety of educational technologies and technology-related teaching strategies and use the findings in districtwide implementation decisions. The model keeps individual investigations small, thereby decreasing the cost (and risk) to the district and increasing its ability to investigate a wider range of innovations.

Additionally, the opportunity to submit proposals has been recognized by many teachers and administrators as a positive and progressive change. The process provides a direct means for teachers interested in a technology application to initiate an investigation into its feasibility. The funding of a proposal serves to recognize that the investigator's idea is of value and enhances his or her perceived status in the school or district.

Of course, there have also been problems with the execution of the process described above. For example, materials ordered for use in investigations have sometimes arrived late and technical problems have occurred, forcing evaluations and recommendations to be delayed until the following year. In one instance, a teacher was awarded an investigation in the spring but was reassigned by fall, and the investigation had to be offered to the replacement. These problems, however, have been greatly outweighed by the benefits.

Future of the Program

The model used by ISD 279 requires that the environment in which the innovation will be investigated is the same one from which the proposal originated. Before becoming involved with the hardware or software, individuals must invest sufficient effort to develop a compelling proposal. This process demonstrates their dedication to the idea and gives them an opportunity to begin acquiring the knowledge necessary to make the investigation successful.

In addition to providing guidance to the district on implementation questions, successful investigations develop an internal pool of experienced, knowledgeable, and usually enthusiastic individuals. These individuals are an invaluable resource during districtwide implementation. At inservice training, their experience and enthusiasm are especially useful in convincing others to make a genuine effort.

The small size of the initial investigations minimizes the damage of unsuccessful investigation in terms of dollars spent and teacher and student time invested. And they are not without benefits even if unsuccessful. Teachers involved in the projects gain from the opportunity to determine how they will teach and the tools they will use, as well as the direction of instruction within the district.

As each year passes, minor revisions are made to streamline and strengthen the investigative model. There is little doubt that this model will continue to be used and evolve as long as it assists the district's administration in making difficult decisions about technology implementation.

References

Fullan, M. (1982). *The Meaning of Educational Change.* New York, N.Y.: Teachers College Press.

Hall, G.E., A.A. George, and W.L. Rutherford. (1979). *Measuring Stages of Concern About the Innovation: A Manual for Use of the SOC Questionnaire.* Austin, Texas: The University of Texas.

Showers, B., B. Joyce, and B. Bennett. (1987). "Synthesis of Research on Staff Development: A Framework for Future Student and a State-of-the-Art Analysis." *Educational Leadership* 45, 3: 77-87.

Stasz, C., and R.J. Shavelson. (1985). "Staff Development for Instructional Uses of Microcomputers." *AEDS Journal* 85: 1-19.

5

Keyboarding: A Necessary Transitional Skill

Gilbert Valdez
Sue Sollie

*I*n a few decades, keyboarding skills may be as obsolete as "proper buggy whip techniques" are today. Already we have developed primitive voice input devices that allow people to use everyday speech to communicate with computers. In a relatively short time, direct voice or even direct-thought communication with computers will be as common and accepted as receiving visual images on television sets. However, until that time, keyboarding must be considered an essential transitional skill that all students should master in order to communicate with machines.

Keyboarding is the ability to effectively use the correct fingers on the correct keys in a manner consistent with practices used by those proficient in using a keyboard to enter information into a computer's memory. Keyboarding increases efficiency in communicating with a computer and reduces personal frustration caused by delay and inaccuracies when entering data. Keyboard practices include the ability to input information without looking at the keys with high accuracy and speed. Keyboarding is distinguished from word processing and typing in that less attention is given to formatting, completing forms,and performing other activities relating to business practices, and more attention is given to entering information efficiently.

Setting Up a Keyboarding Program

School districts that have successful keyboarding programs report that they began with a clear understanding of how keyboarding skills help reinforce desired curriculum and instructional objectives. They used those objectives, in turn, to reinforce the keyboarding skills identified for their keyboarding programs.

Underlying these objectives was the assumption that successful keyboarding instructions help teachers and students feel more empowered and in control of their learning. Technology can help individualize and extend education (see *Educational Leadership*, March *1986* and *Educational Technology*, March 1989 for a more thorough examination of philosophical and inservice issues associated with computers). Effective use of computers assumes individualized interactions with computers that allow efficient input from users. Given the limitations of today's interactive devices, keyboarding remains the major option for interacting with computers.

To ensure that these philosophical ends and educational objectives are served by having students keyboard data into computers, there are several key questions that must be addressed:

- What are the ideal grade levels to introduce keyboarding instruction?
- What should the keyboarding objectives be and how much time should be devoted to keyboarding instruction for students?
- Who should provide the instruction?
- What software should be used with particular students?

What Are the Ideal Grade Levels to Introduce Keyboarding Instruction?

It is interesting to note that the introduction of keyboarding skills **precedes** the personal computer. Sinks and Thurston (1972) found that over 900 studies were made between 1932 and 1972 that consider the impact of typewriters in classroom instruction. Many of those dealt with appropriate grade placement.

Keyboarding should be introduced when students are intellectually, attitudinally, and physically capable of benefiting from the instruction and before computer use requires more than single key interactions that might lead to "hunt and peck" habits. Many researchers and practitioners (Jackson and 1986, Kisner 1984, Rauch and Yanke 1982, Stoecker 1988, and Warwood 1985) agree that the 3rd through 6th grades seem the most appropriate time for beginning formal keyboarding instruction, with 4th grade seeming the most desirable. For instance, Cowles, Hedley, and Robinson (1983) reported that

7- and 8-year olds experienced success and stayed with the keyboarding task. Oksendahl (1972) reported that some students under the age of 10 could type up to 45 words a minute using appropriate keyboarding techniques. Although a number of schools initiate keyboarding at the 4th or 5th grades, many schools have successfully taught keyboarding at the 3rd-grade level and even lower. Classroom teachers at Stevens Creek Elementary School in Cupertino, California, have successfully taught keyboarding to 2nd graders with the aid of Sunburst's *Type to Learn,* which seems well suited to students of that age. By charting their progress, students in the computer-saturated classrooms at Stevens Creek discovered that they could type faster than they could print.

Most educators, however, select the middle grades for keyboarding instruction, because they believe that children in the 3rd through 6th grades have deficient motor skills and lack sustained motivation. There is also an assumption that because students are reading and writing sufficiently well in the middle grades, computer use will accelerate their learning opportunities. Keep in mind that it is at the middle-grade level that students begin to undertake demanding research and writing assignments that require or are significantly enhanced by keyboarding skills. Further, in the various content areas beginning at the middle grades, software is sophisticated enough to require individualized interaction with the computer.

The appropriate time for introducing keyboarding skills should be seen less as a function of age or grade level than the student's need for the skill. There seems to be little point in teaching a skill that students will not have the opportunity to practice in a meaningful way. Much of the available early learning software requires students to enter their name and thereafter respond by single-key presses. In addition, many of the recent copyright software packages for that level take advantage of the mouse-interface of the newer computers, such as the Apple IIGS* and Macintosh, which are becoming increasingly prevalent in the schools. It would seem, then, that keyboarding instruction should coincide with the introduction and use of word processing software.

To wait until the middle grades to develop keyboarding skills, however, risks that students will learn hunt-and-peck techniques that will be extremely difficult to extinguish at a later date. Educators, therefore, should heed the research and plan to introduce keyboarding at about 4th grade.

---

*Apple IIGS is a trademark of Apple Corporation.

What Should the Keyboarding Objectives Be and How Much Time Should Be Devoted to Keyboarding Instruction for Students?

There is no clear agreement among researchers regarding keyboarding objectives and expected speeds. Jackson and Berg (1986) believe that the primary objectives of keyboarding instruction should be the correct manipulation of the alphabetic keyboard and appropriate keyboarding techniques that include body positioning, keystroking, and operation of the space, return, and shift keys. They reported that 30 hours of instruction over a 2- to 3-year period provides the best results. They also suggest that instruction should be in 20- to 30-minute blocks and strongly recommend that only pass/fail grades be given.

Kisner (1984) and the Minnesota Curriculum Services Center (1984) suggest that students be able to type 25 gross words per minute (wpm) before they are considered keyboard competent. Others, such as Wetzel (1985), believe that goals should be as low as 10 wpm, because keyboarding instruction, although important, should be practiced in the context of the existing curriculum. Approximately 12 hours in 30-minute blocks over a year should be devoted specifically to keyboarding instruction, according to Wetzel.

Who Should Provide the Instruction?

Jackson and Berg (1986) indicate that either elementary or high school typing teachers could provide instruction if they have a high interest in teaching keyboarding and have taken methods courses in keyboarding and appropriate courses that help them in working with elementary students. This does not preclude other teachers and professionals who have sufficient keyboarding training.

What Software Should Be Used with Particular Students?

Keyboarding software must be motivating and provide positive reinforcement. Knapp (1984) recommends the following additional characteristics of quality keyboarding software:

1. Throughout the program, frequent feedback about typing accuracy and speed should be given.
2. The program should display upper- and lower-case letters, and the user should be able to recognize the difference when searching for errors.
3. Error corrections should be possible while typing the exercises.
4. Students should be able to escape from a lesson and return to a menu at any time without having to reboot the system.
5. The program should provide space for teacher-created exercises.

6. The user should be able to establish the words-per-minute goal as part of the time drill.

7. The program should provide a management system that keeps track of students' progress.

8. The program should allow students to select exercises that focus on speed, accuracy, or both.

9. The program should contain an appropriate vocabulary for the grade levels for which it will be used.

The keyboarding software on the market runs the gamut from arcade-style drills designed to improve the speed of individuals who already have keyboarding skills to complete packages that begin with the correct placement of the fingers on the keyboard. Some recent additions to the keyboarding software market include packages that employ some elements of artificial intelligence. *Mavis Beacon Teaches Typing* by Software Toolworks is an example of this new genre of keyboarding software. However, software choices will depend on a number of factors, including hardware compatibility, cost, licensing arrangements, the number of computers available, the presence of a hard-disk-based network, and the skill of the instructor.

Case Study: Blue Earth, Minnesota

The Blue Earth Public School in rural Blue Earth, Minnesota, a K-12 school, foresaw the importance of developing keyboarding skills as a precursor to using the computer effectively as a writing tool. In 1981, the school developed a comprehensive plan for integrating technology into the educational process, which, among other goals, called for the development of minimum keyboarding proficiencies at the elementary school level. Students had their first contact with computers and began keyboard familiarization activities in kindergarten. Formal keyboard instruction was introduced as the students began to move beyond traditional computer-assisted-instructional (CAI) activities to use the computers for word processing.

In 1984, many of the goals of the technology implementation plan were realized in the establishment of an experimental, technology-rich classroom at the 4th grade level. In this classroom, each student had access to a computer at a workstation. If the students were to make the most efficient use of the technology available to them, it was imperative that they develop some competency with keyboarding skills. To this end, a business education teacher was hired to teach keyboarding skills in an intensive, two-week course in which the students were instructed in two 45-minute sessions per day. Daily half-hour sessions followed for the next six weeks. At the end of that time, students were touch typing at speeds of 30 wpm and up. Keyboarding skills were practiced throughout the year via occasional speed drills and extensive use of the skill during writing activities.

The success of the 4th grade students in the experimental classroom removed all doubts concerning the appropriateness of teaching keyboarding at that level and raised a new question: If 4th graders could readily develop keyboarding proficiency, could 3rd graders as well? With the establishment of additional technology-rich classrooms and the increased availability of computers for all students, the Blue Earth School launched a keyboarding skills program in 1985 for all students in grades 3, 4, 5, and 6. The program, which was considered to be successful, continues today with few modifications.

A Closer Look at the Program's Activities

Beginning in kindergarten, under the direction of classroom teachers, students are first introduced to the computers through keyboard familiarization activities, charts, and picture keyboards. *The Friendly Computer* from the Minnesota Educational Computing Corporation (MECC) is the software of choice, partially because MECC products are available through a cost-effective licensing arrangement at the school. No emphasis is placed on correct fingering, since the software used by students at this level generally requires single keypress responses.

Formal keyboarding instruction begins in 3rd grade, with additional instruction and reinforcement continuing into grades 4, 5, and 6. Reinforcement includes reviewing keyboarding techniques when creating databases in social studies classes and creative writing in language arts classes. The high school business education teacher assists individual students. The classroom teacher, while not responsible for keyboarding instruction, is expected to reinforce appropriate keyboarding techniques during practice sessions and when the students are engaged in activities, such as word processing, which require the use of the skill. The business education teacher chose to use the elementary keyboarding textbook from Southwestern Publishing, coupled with a word processor that gives the students a blank screen on which to practice. Also available for keyboarding practice and review are a variety of software programs that include *The Wonderful World of Paws* from Southwestern Publishing, the MECC keyboarding series, *type!* from Broderbund, and *Tut's Typer* from Roger Wagner Publishing Company. The choice of software is limited to products from companies that are willing to make reasonable licensing arrangements for multiple copies of their software and the school's network's ability to use the software.

Scheduling of Instruction

Third-grade students learn the use of all keys, including keys that are peculiar to computers, during a nine-week period. Students receive 15 minutes of instruction from the business education teacher, followed by 15 minutes of practice time under the supervision of their classroom teacher 3 times per week.

Time for the keyboarding instruction is taken from the language arts curriculum block since the skills are deemed necessary for writing. Once students have acquired some proficiency with keyboarding skills, classroom teachers are expected to provide the opportunities for students to exercise those skills by initiating word processing activities.

Third-grade keyboarding is followed by a nine-week refresher at the beginning of fourth grade, four weeks in fifth grade, and two weeks in sixth grade. Keyboarding instruction is optional beyond that point and not available again until ninth grade. Students who enter the school for their first time are placed in the keyboarding class currently in progress.

Personnel

The choice of a business education teacher for keyboarding instruction forestalled two difficulties often encountered when implementing elementary keyboarding programs. First, the elementary teachers were not required to teach a skill they may not have mastered themselves; second, the high school business education department supported the program because they were assured of its integrity.

In many instances, such an arrangement with the business teacher is impossible or, at best, difficult. Business education teachers frequently oppose elementary keyboarding and bemoan the prospect of rectifying improperly taught skills when the students reach high school. While reality frequently dictates that the teaching of keyboarding skills falls to elementary classroom teachers, computer teachers, or computer lab supervisors, it is advisable to seek the support and involvement of the high school business education department to whatever degree possible.

Business education teachers can also assist in the implementation of elementary keyboarding programs by becoming involved in the selection of the software and textbooks that will be used. They can also hold workshops for individuals who will teach the keyboarding classes, instructing them on appropriate techniques and methodologies. These classes are particularly useful for teachers who have never enrolled in a typing course or who have not participated in a typing/keyboarding course since high school.

* * *

Keyboarding will be an obsolete skill in our students' lifetimes. However, until technological developments are perfected and schools can afford these new tools for communicating with computers, keyboarding remains an essential skill. Certainly, the alternative— students ineffectively and inefficiently interacting with machines in a hunt-and-peck manner—is undesirable. Schools need to provide students with appropriate instruction that will allow them to interact efficiently with computers. Otherwise, they will be at a great disadvantage compared with students who can use the keyboard.

References

Cowles, M., M. Hedley, and M.C. Robinson. (1983). *An Analysis of Young Children Learning Keyboarding Skills*. Birmingham: University of Alabama-Birmingham, School of Education.

Jackson, T.H., and D. Berg (March 1986). "Elementary Keyboarding-Is It Important?" *The Computing Teacher* 13: 70-715.

Kisner, E. (February 1984). "Keyboarding—A Must in Tomorrow's World." *The Computing Teacher* 11, 6: 21-22.

Knapp, L.R. (1984). "Finding the Best Typing Tutorials." *Classroom Computer Learning* 70-715.

Minnesota Curriculum Services Center. (1984). "The Electronic Keyboard for Personal and Business Use." St. Paul, Minn. : Minnesota Curriculum Services.

Oksendahl, W.J. (1972). "Keyboard Literacy for Hawaii's Primary Children." *Education Horizon* 51, 4: 20-27.

Rauch, V., and P. Young. (December 1982). "Keyboarding in Kindergarten—Is It Elementary?" *Business Education Forum* 19-22.

Sinks, T.A., and J.F Thurston. (1972). "Effects of Typing on School Achievement in Elementary Grades." Paper presented at the Educational Computing Conference - NECCC 88 in Dallas, Texas.

Stoecker, J.W. (1988). "Teacher Training for Keyboarding Instruction—Grades 4-8: A Researched and Field Tested Inservice Model." Paper presented at the National Educational Computing Conference—NECC 88 in Dallas, Texas.

Warwood, B. (1985). "A Research Study to Determine the Effects of Early Keyboard Use Upon Student Development in Occupational Keyboarding." Final Report of Research. Bozeman, Montana: Montana State University. ERIC, ED 265 367.

Wetzel, K. (1985). "Keyboarding Skills—Elementary, My Dear Teacher." *The Computing Teacher* 15-19.

6

Interactive Information Systems

Frank B. Withrow

*W*ith technological innovations, there is always a trade off between old and new. Educational decision makers must carefully weigh such benefits and costs when considering the introduction of a new technology to improve learning. It is particularly critical to weigh benefits and costs when considering the use of interactive information systems. Defined here as technologies that enable learners to act on audio, visual, and textual information at their own pace, these systems provide teachers and students with cost-effective educational resources.

A Closer Look at the Systems

Among the most exciting of the new interactive information systems are components of optical storage systems:

- Videodisc,
- Compact Disc Read Only Memory (CD-ROM),
- Digital Video Interactive (DVI), and
- Compact Disc Interactive (CD-I) technologies.

The standard 12-inch laser videodisc can store 54,000 single-frame pictures on each side. Each picture is accessible in seconds and can be played as full-motion colored sequences with stereo sound. Coupled with a computer, such interactive systems can enter into a dialogue with the learner. Even without the computer control, such systems offer the teacher and student access to a large, visual database. The combination of these programs with CD-ROM systems offers a new configuration of learning technology with a wide range of demonstrated industrial training applications, from basic electronic courses to management courses.

A number of interactive programs in science and mathematics have been used in elementary and secondary education. While these technologies are not yet widespread, there is a growing awareness of them, and a number of new programs are being developed in the United States and England.

Some of the first applications of these technologies were much like reference books that displayed print, colored pictures, audio information, full motion sound, and simulations of real experiences. And characteristics have since expanded. Users can now

- either compress or expand events in time,
- view dramatizations of recreated historical events (in some cases, actual footage of 20th-century events are available),
- control simulations of dangerous or violent events, and
- make micro and macro examinations of events and experiences.

For example, an internal combustion engine can be explored through an animated voyage through its cycles of operation. The learner can direct the speed of the voyage and call upon stored information to supplement the animations.

Ultimately, as the technologies develop, they have the potential for cost reduction. For instance, the 1989 price for the regular print version of *Grollier Encyclopedia* was $800, but the price was only $80 for the videodisc version and $200 for the CD-ROM version. It is also expected that as these systems become integral parts of home television and communications systems, with the average citizen having access to these bodies of stored knowledge, costs will decrease accordingly.

What Happens in the Classroom?

One of the great challenges facing educators in the next few years is how to integrate these technologies into typical classroom routines. Or better still, how to use these systems to extend students' learning. In the largest sense, they represent tools that can enhance the content of the curriculum—tools that both teachers and students can use to refine and develop their understanding of a subject area.

Many products are currently available or under study that illustrate the use of these systems to enhance learning. One example of this is a product on bioscience developed by Joe Clark, President of Video Discovery, Inc. At the fingertip of either the teacher or student on the *Bioscience* disc are slides with animated sequences on DNA and actual motion sequences on cell division. Teachers and students can use this resource daily, looking up references to bioscience questions as they would in a traditional reference book. With these materials, teachers and students are able to examine in detail the micro and macro aspects of bioscience.

The development of laser videodiscs, CD-ROM, and various interfaces with computers, such as HyperCard, enable users to index, file, and retrieve a massive amount of data. Such systems move back and forth from print to picture to motion to sound and various combinations with maximum ease.

An example of this type of hyper screen capability is being developed experimentally by Apple Computer, Inc. and Scholastic, Inc., using videodisc and the HyperCard. Such relational databases allow the user to track through the system in an infinite array of paths that include such things as the *Federalist Papers*, excerpts from the Contra Hearings, historical footage from newsreels, and countless still photographs and drawings. A student can even explore prepared explanations of the Civil War from the viewpoints of President Lincoln or Robert E. Lee.

IBM, using their InfoWindo system, developed a similar product for exhibition during the celebration of the 200 years of the Constitution. Their database includes many items related to the Constitution, in addition to items relevant to issues of today.

*　　*　　*

Years ago, we could expect our teachers to be all-knowing resources of information. Today, in a given subject area, the knowledge explosion is so fast that even leading experts have difficulty assimilating the developments. Therefore, teachers must have tools at hand to help students acquire the knowledge and experiences needed to master specific content areas. It is important to remember that 90 percent of all of the scientists the world has ever known are alive today. No scientist today, whether medical doctor or research physicist, can hope to keep up with developments without life-long learning.

The challenge of teaching and learning in the next century will be to know how to seek out information, how to ask the relevant questions, how to use this information to express new ideas, and how to find the resources available to each user. It is essential that our schools join with all other aspects of society in increasing their productivity through appropriate applications of technology.

The most disadvantaged in the 21st century will be those whose access to inter-active information systems is limited or nonexistent.

References

Interactive Videodiscs—A Directory for Educators. (1986). Chelmsford, Mass.: Merrimack Educational Center.

The Videodisc Compendium for Education and Training. (1989). St. Paul, Minn.: Emerging Technology Consultants Inc.

Planning for Telecommunications: A School Leader's Primer. (1989). Alexandria, Va.: National School Boards Association.

7

Using Computer-Assisted Instruction to Support Learners

Glenn H. Crumb

*I*n recent years, educators, parents, and the public have asked about the relationship between computers and educational goals. Practitioners have become informed consumers who demand reliable, valid courseware that is error free and "user friendly." Their sophistication also leads them to seek courseware that makes appropriate use of sound learning principles, productive teaching methods, and accurate content. The power of the computer is being used to provide support for content instruction, management for learning, and documentation of both time on task and learner achievement. Finally, and perhaps most significantly, the computer's use is being expanded to include helping the teacher apply diagnostic-prescriptive teaching practices that use the time of both teacher and learner more efficiently. Computer-assisted instruction (CAI) is giving the educator a tool to increase educational effectiveness and provide accountability.

Many schools find the costs of quality CAI software too high. Although numerous systems for developing one's own software are now available, developing and producing quality CAI software is still quite costly. But, as in the case of hardware purchasing decisions, the real cost lies in selecting poor software. Educators must determine that software meets content validity, has a good learning design, is error free, and is appropriate for the grade and age level of the user. Many programs are available on floppy disks in a wide range of school subject areas.

Advantages to Using CAI

When looking at the time investment and cost factors, educators must examine the "trade offs." There are some definite advantages to using CAI. A brief summary of these advantages, which many practitioners believe offset the costs, follows.

Improved Achievement

Bangert-Drowns, Kulik, and Kulik (1985) and many others have conducted meta-analysis of research studies on CAI effectiveness and found that students receiving CAI scored better on standardized achievement tests than did their peers who received no CAI. They also found that CAI-taught students had better retention and that CAI improved the speed at which students learned a given amount of material.

Two inferences follow from this research. First, CAI can make learners' time on task more efficient. Given the rate at which knowledge is increasing, more efficient learning grows in importance as each year passes. Second, educators and researchers should try to identify hardware and software that specifically leverages the power of the computer, not only to provide instruction but also to meet the specific needs of the learner. As the search for more effective and efficient means of learning continues, the computer can become an effective tool for data collection to document the information needed to test various instructional models and their costs.

Data collected from projects conducted in a variety of school settings (including California, Kentucky, Louisiana, and Massachusetts) provide evidence of class-average achievement gains of more than 1 year for every 25 hours of time on task, consisting of computer-generated drill and practice in reading or mathematics. The students in these models received ten minutes of CAI time on task each school day, with teachers providing individualized concept instruction based on diagnostic-prescriptive information generated by the computer. Students were involved in at least one teacher-reported, motivational CAI activity each semester. The hardware used to deliver the CAI included either terminals connected to microcomputers or stand-alone microcomputers. In most cases, school sites were connected by telephone or microwave systems to a centrally located minicomputer.

The costs of communications, courseware, hardware, and system mainte-nance appear, at first, to be beyond the reach of most schools. But given the achievement gains they reported, the ability to document student progress at will, and the high efficiency of mastery achievement, the costs may well be less than investing in hardware and courseware on floppy disks that have none of these advantages.

Expansion of Services

Schools using centrally located mainframe systems and programs have dis-covered other advantages. After school hours and during summer months, the CAI network has been used to provide basic skills instruction in adult educa-tion programs. Evidence (Nickols 1987) indicates that providing learners with as little as three or four weeks of intensive summer access to CAI, using ele-ments of the model cited previously, yields close to three-fourths of a year of mastery achievement in basic skills. The Jefferson County (Kentucky) Schools, for instance, are opening a new school for those still of school age but who are out of school and without a high school diploma. The school will operate pri-marily at night, use mastery learning strategies, award Carnegie units toward the high school diploma, be entirely individualized, and make heavy use of CAI to provide instructional support.

The multiple uses of hardware not only reduce overall costs for instruc-tional services, but also provide insight into how computers can be used to deliver productive learning activities. Still other benefits include the ability to

- centrally administer the analysis and reporting of mastery achievement,
- provide for administrative communication through electronic mail, and
- meet the instructional needs of homebound students using dial-up access to the computer.

At this time, these administrative capabilities are being used in a limited way, but there are indications that further expansion will occur as more admin-istrators become aware of the power and availability of such resources.

Networking and Cooperative Systems

With advances in computer and communications technologies, the ability to tap into substantial amounts of computer power for classroom use at a rea-sonable cost continues to grow. Cooperative CAI networks are one example. A cooperative CAI network in Kentucky consists of a consortium of 24 public schools and a comprehensive university, which share the administrative, hardware, courseware, maintenance, and communications costs of CAI. The cost per school year in 1988 for services to 25-50 middle school students was about $900. From this service, a student gets an excellent opportunity to gain more than one year of achievement in mathematics or reading skills as a result of drill and practice used with a planned program of concept teaching (Crumb 1988).

In one rural middle school of the network cited above, the average CAI math gains exceeded 2.15 years for 62 Chapter I students who had an average of 20.23 hours of time on task (Crumb 1988). After two years of using the program, this school is reporting no students eligible for Chapter I mathematics, with only incoming students needing remediation. The average cost to the school per year of CAI achievement gain was $42.10 per student. At another isolated rural school, 36 students have access to CAI for just ten minutes per day. These students had an average mastery achievement gain of 1.84 years at a cost of $26.43 per student per year.

The number of telephone and microwave communication networks to support remote classroom sites has been growing rapidly since the early 1980s. More rapid and reliable modems, improved telephone systems, and the application of new and sophisticated computer communications technology have provided more school systems a cost-effective means to network CAI programs. The development of better and less expensive microwave systems and more efficient use of those already in place have also added to cost-effectiveness.

In south central Kentucky, a group of seven school districts shares a network that provides CAI in basic skills (reading, mathematics, and language arts). The network consists of a state-owned microwave and telephone lines that connect a minicomputer at Western Kentucky University with remote classrooms at distances of up to 100 miles. The CAI is available at some sites for both day and night school applications. Electronic mail is used routinely to communicate among classroom teachers, administrators, and university personnel. The network has operated since 1984 and has proven to be effective in supporting learners and their teachers.

Looking Ahead

The use of computers in schools will expand as their effectiveness and place in instruction, classroom management, and administration become better understood by educational decision makers. The critical role of the teacher is in interpreting how new technology can be used for productive teaching and learning. There must be a synergistic interlocking of technology as a relevant part of the curriculum if it is to be used effectively. Teachers must be comfortable with technology, use it for their own learning, and have the support that allows them to make maximum applications of the technology resources available in specific content areas.

Mature systems for education will focus on content and learner mastery of that content. Time will not be the fixed basis for education with mastery flexible for individual students, but mastery criteria standards will be fixed and time will be flexible. The essence of educational technology is the appropriate use of human and nonhuman resources to change the learner's behavior so that new skills are developed, new knowledge is acquired, and performance meets an agreed-on level of acceptance.

The tools are available, and the challenge is great; the question is how educators will adapt to the needs of an information-rich society. The American educational system, with its mix of private and public education, enabled us to dominate the economic and industrial world during the last part of the industrial age. The challenge facing us now is to accommodate the needs of the information age and not look back. I think that we will meet this challenge.

References

Bangert-Drowns, R.L., J.A. Kulik, and C.-L.C. Kulik. (April 1985). "Effectiveness of Computer-Based Education in Secondary Schools." Paper presented at the annual meeting of the American Educational Research Association, Chicago.

Clement, C., D.M. Kurland, R. Mawby, and R.D. Pea. (In press). "Analogical Reasoning and Computer Programming." *Journal of Educational Computing Research*.

Crumb, G.H. (July 1988). "Computer-Assisted Instruction Achievement Gains versus Time-On-Task and Cost Analysis: An Annual Report." Professional Center Network Consortium Meeting. Western Kentucky University.

"Effectiveness of the CAI Program for Chapter I Students in Fort Worth Parochial Schools 1986-87." Fort Worth Independent School District, Fort Worth, TX. (See also a similar report for 1985-86).

Hatard, S., and J.C. Marion. (August 1987). "Evaluation of Lafayette Parish Job Training Summer Remedial Program." Presented to Lafayette Parish School Board and Lafayette Parish Job Training Department.

Hawkins, J., and D.M. Kurland. (1984). "Analysis of Software Tools." Report to the Carnegie Corporation. New York: Bank Street College of Education, Center for Children and Technology.

Hawkins, J., C. Char, and C. Freeman. (1984). "Software Tools in the Classroom." Report to the Carnegie Corporation. New York: Bank Street College of Education, Center for Children and Technology.

Hawkins, J., R. Mawby, and M. Ghitman. (In press). "Practices of Novices and Experts in Critical Inquiry." In *Minors of Minds*, edited by R.D. Pea and K. Sheingold. Norwood, N.J.: Abex.

Kulik, J.A., C.-L.C. Kulik, and R.L. Bangert-Drowns. (April 1985). "Effectiveness of Computer-Based Education in Elementary Schools." Paper presented at the annual meeting of the American Educational Research Association, Chicago.

Levin, H.M. "Cost Effectiveness of Computer-Assisted Instruction: Proceedings of the International Conference on Courseware Design and Evaluation." Ramert Gua, Israel: Israel Association for Computers in Education.

Nickols, S. (July 1987). "Achievement Gains In Summer Programs Using CAI." Private Communication: Glasgow Middle School, Glasgow, Ky.

Pea, R.D., and D.M. Kurland. "On the Cognitive Prerequisites of Learning Computer Programming." Report to the National Institute for Research in Education, U.S. Office of Education (Contract #400-83-0016).

Pea, R.D., D.M. Kurland, and J. Hawkins. (1985). "Logo Programming and Development of Thinking Skills." In *Children and Microcomputers: Formative Studies*, edited by M. Chen and W. Parsley. Beverley Hills, Calif.: Sage.

Ragosta, M., and D. Jamison. (June 1982). "Computer-Assisted Instructional and Compensatory Education." The Executive Summary and Policy Implications. Princeton, N.J.: Educational Testing Service (Project Report Number 20).

8

On-Line Computer Databases in School Library Media Centers

Carol C. Kuhlthau
Joyce C. Sherman

*T*oday's students will function as adults in a milieu where access to unlimited amounts of information from electronic sources will be commonplace, and the efficient and creative management of this information may well be the crucial ingredient. Students must become familiar with the new means of accessing information as easily and quickly as possible, so they can move on to the creative uses of the information.

On-line databases are becoming a basic resource for library collections. They fill a void that has traditionally existed in school libraries — the lack of truly current information. On-line databases also make available vast amounts of materials that are either difficult or impossible to locate in other sources. Additionally, the entire school population can have access to the resource when it is placed in the library media center.

Vendors currently market several databases to schools. Examples include:

- Dialog — a command-driven information retrieval system of 300 databases with sophisticated research capability.
- Compuserv — a consumer-oriented, menu-driven information retrieval service.
- Dow Jones News/Retrieval System— a wide variety of general databases as well as extensive, detailed corporate and industrial information.

51

What follows is a description of how the South Brunswick (New Jersey) School District integrated the Dow Jones News/Retrieval System into their educational program.

Since January 1985, Brunswick Acres School, a K-6 elementary school in South Brunswick Township, has been using the Dow Jones News/Retrieval System, an electronic information service. News/Retrieval is an integrated service consisting of more than 35 distinct databases, among them:

- the full texts of *The Wall Street Journal* and *The Washington Post*,
- an electronic encyclopedia (updated quarterly),
- up-to-the minute news and sports coverage,
- current weather information from around the world and movie reviews (for films made in 1926 to present),
- a college selection service,
- a medical and drug reference,
- the *Official Airline Guide*,
- book reviews, and
- an on-line shopping service.

In addition, there are numerous financially related databases.

Program Background

Brunswick Acres School was introduced to News/Retrieval as part of a pilot project involving four school districts in central New Jersey. Two of the many questions explored by the pilot project were whether an elementary school was an educationally appropriate setting for an on-line database system and whether placing the system in the library media center would work. After 18 months of experience, the South Brunswick Board of Education was sufficiently convinced of the value of electronic databases in the elementary setting to have funded their placement in all the elementary schools, as well as the middle school and the high school library media centers.

The News/Retrieval database is particularly appropriate for school library media centers because the information is relevant to many areas of the elementary and secondary curriculum. The information available can be readily applied to classroom learning without wasting time on inconsequential, distracting material. Another advantage of News/Retrieval is a flat-rate charge—per password, per year—making it possible for a school system to budget accurately.

It is not necessary to be computer literate to use News/Retrieval successfully. Students only have to know how to type on the keyboard. They quickly learn everything else through prompts from the program itself. Brunswick Acres 2nd graders studying Alaska checked the temperatures of Alaskan cities on the terminal and used the information to construct a daily weather graph.

Electronic databases have proven to be a great motivator for children who might be reluctant to use print resources. The experience at Brunswick Acres has shown that the currency and relevance of information on News/Retrieval is highly motivating to students of all ages and ability levels. Using an electronic source of information, even the most reluctant learners seem to experience a sense of mastery, leading to greater participation in the management of their own learning.

Educational Goals

In considering the needs of the learner and the educational goals of the teacher, two major learning objectives were identified:

- to develop skill and confidence using electronic information
- to develop critical thinking skills needed to handle information.

Literacy goes beyond reading to the ability to access and use information. Information use involves not only locating but analyzing, summarizing, paraphrasing, synthesizing, and presenting to others. News/Retrieval has proven effective for developing skill in using electronic information. Children using the system become comfortable with the technology and confident in their ability to access information. They learn about what kind of information is available and become aware of how they can meet their own information needs through the use of on-line databases. Through experience and practice, they find out that the computer database is a tool for learning and decision making.

Critical thinking skills have been enhanced as well through using the on-line retrieval system. Critical thinking skills and information-use skills are developed naturally through activities that lead children to think critically about the information they locate. Critical analysis involves an understanding of opinion and bias. Children learn to make comparisons between different approaches to an issue. They become aware of editorial judgments made in the inclusion and exclusion of news items. They also develop skills in problem solving and decision making based on the information retrieved in their investigations.

Activities to Support Learning

Two kinds of activities using News/Retrieval have been developed. Some were designed to be used by individual students as they become familiar with the technology. For example, in "Racing to Win," a hypothetical one-mile race between a cheetah, a greyhound, and Roger Bannister, the man who first ran a mile in under four minutes, students are required to:

- define terms such as win, place, and show,
- obtain information from several sources,
- compare meters and miles by converting numbers, and
- solve time and distance problems.

Other activities were designed to extend and enrich curriculum-related topics. Access to current information breathed new life into some old classroom exercises. A biography unit, for example, no longer produced a classroom of students writing a thinly disguised, plagiarized report on an assigned historical figure. Instead, students worked on an activity called "A Chapter in the Life of..." using current news stories to write biographical material about someone whose life is still unfolding in the pages of today's newspapers. As students gather information from primary sources, they gain a greater understanding of how biography differs from other forms of writing and expand their ability to evaluate the relative importance of factual information.

Studying explorers becomes an adventure when students use the *Official Airline Guide* and the *Academic American Encyclopedia* on line, along with the standard reference sources and maps, to follow the travels of Christopher Columbus or Lewis and Clark and then chart a modern airplane tour following the same route. Comparisons of elapsed travel time use mathematical skills and relevant geographical concepts are learned in a meaningful context.

In "The Rain in Spain" activity, students use the weather and encyclopedia databases, along with other resources, to collect and analyze information about the relationship between location and weather. Data about four cities located at similar latitudes are compiled and graphed. Variations are noted and hypotheses formulated about the relationship between temperature and location. Students are required to do additional research to draw conclusions and make comparisons about the data obtained.

News/Retrieval enables the user to approach a topic from a variety of viewpoints. For example, a current environmental issue might be explored from governmental, legal, health, industry-wide, and specific corporate points of view—all without leaving the terminal. When a 5th grader became ill with chicken pox, a fellow student became concerned. The student recalled that taking aspirin when one has the chicken pox could cause complications. The student tapped into MDEX, News/Retrieval's medical and drug reference, and discovered that the combination of aspirin and chicken pox could lead to the fatal Reyes Syndrome. Another student picked up on the business aspect of the aspirin/chicken pox combination to determine how the news affected stock prices of drug companies.

News/Retrieval is also being used extensively at South Brunswick High School. A chemistry teacher testifies that the teaching of periodic tables has been converted from one of the dullest exercises of the year to one of constant surprises. Students are assigned an element and told to find out all they can about it using News/Retrieval. One student, assigned the element fluorine, found out that just a week earlier, a derivative of the element had been used in new ways to change the composition of racing car tires and in the process of making artificial blood. A student gaining this kind of information is likely to be motivated to a greater extent than a student reading about fluorine's past application in a textbook.

Finally, there is an obvious excitement when it becomes possible to follow a fast-breaking news story as it happens. The old standby—current events—takes on new meaning. The News/Retrieval database provides information from the wire services with only a 90-second delay. The explosion of the Challenger and the incident at Chernobyl could be followed by students from moment to moment.

Implementation

The integration of this resource into the educational program has been most successful when initiated by the library media specialist. They can conduct inservice workshops to familiarize teachers with the system. The most effective approach, however, has been for the library media specialist to initiate a project with a particular teacher — a project in which planning, teaching, and oversight are shared equally.

Teachers and library media specialists involved in the pilot project have compiled a manual of activities, based on their collective experiences, to be used in conjunction with News/Retrieval for primary grades through high school. The manual is available from Dow Jones as part of their service. These activities are merely a jumping-off point. The ways News/Retrieval can implement and enrich the school curriculum are numerous.

* * *

In summary, an electronic database puts vast amounts of current and historical information at students' fingertips. The search for background and context is often transformed from a chore into an adventurous journey. Students spend less time locating and recording information and more time analyzing what they have found. The emphasis in planning teaching units can be placed on higher-level thinking skills. Teachers can ask questions requiring more judgment, evaluation, and thought. Interrelationships, previously unnoticed, emerge between subjects under study and current political, economic, government, science, and environmental news. Information delivered through telecommunications is highly motivating to students. Today's world is truly brought into the school.

9

Telecommunications: Using Phone Lines in the Classroom

Denis Newman

A few years ago, it was almost unheard of to have telephone lines in classrooms. Now, lines are being installed in computer labs, libraries, resource rooms, and other classrooms. But it is not that teachers are finding more time to chat on the phone. In fact, often there is no phone in the room. Instead, teachers are using the familiar modular jack for their computers. The computer is becoming a popular communications device, linking teachers and students to the world outside the classroom.

The number of applications of telecommunications continues to grow. Students are writing on word processors then transmitting the files as electronic mail to students in other schools. Science classes are calling up weather services to obtain up-to-the-minute information about weather patterns for the whole country. And teachers are sending electronic mail queries to teachers all around the country to find solutions to specific problems.

As the cost and technical barriers continue to drop, many school systems are making phone lines available in classrooms and computer labs. This chapter gives some examples of how telecommunications is being used in education. It also addresses the change in the use of telecommunications from hobby to institutionalized instructional tool for teachers.

Getting Started

To get started in telecommunications you need a microcomputer, communications software, and a small device called a "modem," which serves as the standard modular jack. You may also need membership in some "host" computer you plan to call up (CompuServe, The Source, or Dow Jones, for example). If your school district already runs a computer bulletin board system then a separate membership is usually not needed, just the phone number. With the membership, you usually get a list of phone numbers in or near your local calling area that you can use to access information. (An excellent overview of the technology and the services available is found in Glossbrenner 1986).

With the technology in place, there are a variety of ways it can be used to promote student learning. The fundamental notion in all the applications of telecommunications is that they bring the world into the classroom. The classroom is literally connected to the outside world—an audience for student writing becomes available and numerous sources of up-to-the-minute information are on line.

When the classroom computer is connected to a phone line it enables teachers and students to call other computers—in the next room or another school, state, or country. Part of the complexity of telecommunications arises from the fact that users not only have to know how to operate the software on their own computers in order to make contact with the other computer but they also have to know how to operate the computer they are calling. While making contact with, and actually operating, a computer one has never seen may be intimidating to some people, there is a thrill in realizing that the familiar classroom computer is a gateway to a much larger world in this information age. And it is not just other computers one is making contact with, it is also other people. Other people call the same computers to leave electronic mail, articles they or their students have written, public domain computer programs that others can copy, and notices about important events.

Some connections can be made via conventional means, of course. For example, it would be foolish to pay an hourly charge to have students search a computerized version of an encyclopedia when the same material is available in the school library. Other kinds of databases, ones that are very volatile, for example weather information or information on natural disasters, are more appropriate for on-line classroom use because they give the students a sense of involvement in the events as they occur. Similarly, if newspaper stories and editorials are being shared between only two classrooms, the conventional mail system (even for sending a floppy disk) may be simpler and cheaper, although somewhat slower, than telecommunications. However, if a larger network of classrooms are sharing their writing, it becomes far simpler to "broadcast" a copy of the message to all the sites simultaneously. In general, the connection to the outside world via telecommunications is most effective when the information is timely and when there are a significant number of students or classrooms involved in the activity.

The Bank Street College Experience with Telecommunications

Examples of telecommunications activities illustrate additional principles for the effective use of technology in education. Over the last three years, several projects at Bank Street College have used telecommunications to provide teacher support in two national training projects: the IBM Model Schools Project (for more information see Newman and Rehfield 1985) and the Mathematics, Science and Technology Teacher Education (MASTTE) project (McGinnis 1986). Also, in the Bank Street Exchange project, we set up our own bulletin board system for use by Bank Street staff and students in the School for Children as well as teachers and students in the neighborhood. Another project, Earth Lab, integrated several levels of communication— among students in a school, among schools in a neighborhood, and among cities around the world (Newman 1987).

The Mathematics, Science and Technology Teacher Education (MASTTE) project focused on improving math, science, and technology education in upper elementary grades (Quinsaat, Friel, and McCarthy 1985). The particular focus was on a multimedia (TV, software, and print) package called *The Voyage of the Mimi*. Teachers and district support personnel from around the country spent two weeks at Bank Street receiving training on the content, pedagogy, planning, and management related to the materials. Follow-up support included site visits by the training staff as well as telecommunications between the training staff and the participating teachers. For the latter, we used The Source, one of the largest commercial services, which can be accessed from any major city.

Because this was a training project, our initial idea was to use telecommunications primarily for conveying information about the materials and providing ideas on how they could be used. The network served this function moderately well. However, the most popular use of telecommunications was a classroom activity. We invited several "guest experts," scientists and other experts featured in the TV show, to field questions from the students. Classroom time was spent in discussions of what the students would ask each of the experts and later in reading and discussing the answers that were received. The enthusiasm for this activity, confirmed by the results of a survey of the teachers, convinced us to reverse our original strategy. Instead of using telecommunications to provide information about the materials and a forum for discussion of issues and problems related to science education, we decided to put an emphasis on the use of telecommunications for classroom activities.

The project provided individualized support for the teachers in several ways. Teachers often asked, "What can I do in the classroom?" Our strategy directly provided support by creating interesting classroom activities. Once the value of the medium is demonstrated to teachers in this way, the secondary functions of providing information and a forum for discussion of issues follow naturally as needed.

One unique form of teacher support was found in the guest expert series. One of the pedagogical goals of the MASTTE project was to help teachers feel more comfortable about not knowing all the answers to the science questions students may raise. Having the guest experts on line allowed teachers to rely on them for immediate answers, turning some potentially uncomfortable moments into occasions for productive classroom dialogue.

The Bank Street Exchange, another telecommunications project at Bank Street, is providing a variety of writing activities for students in neighboring schools. Some of these were modelled on similar activities pioneered by Jim Levin, Margaret Riel, and their colleagues (Levin, Riel, Rowe, and Boruta 1985; Riel 1985). Essentially, the Exchange is a bulletin board system running on a microcomputer at Bank Street. Several classes at neighboring elementary schools used the Exchange quite regularly. The Exchange was open to the public and we received calls form around the country once word got out in the "underground" bulletin board community. Some interesting communications occurred between children who called the Exchange from their home computer after hearing about it through the grapevine. It was very clear from the kinds of unintended exchanges that began on the Exchange that bulletin boards are part of a computer culture with a life quite independent of schools.

Bulletin board operators (called "sysops," short for systems operators) take great pride in their boards and the services they provide. In many respects, telecommunications is still predominantly a hobbyist activity as other microcomputer activities were six years ago. In moving toward more widespread and professional use of the medium, we must remember that a bulletin board can be a source of pride for a school or school district. The person who takes on the job of sysop should begin the task with sufficient enthusiasm to get through some of the technical complexities that can be encountered. While it helps the sysop to have a bit of a hobbyist attitude, it also helps to have sufficient release time to do a job the school or district will be proud of.

Many of the long distance pen pal messages on the Exchange were arranged between our Bank Street staff and our colleagues in the San Diego area. Using a process we call a "portage," we transferred messages that the students in New York wrote from the Exchange to The Source (the national network) and our colleagues in San Diego portaged the messages from The Source to their local system. Answers from students in San Diego were then portaged back to The Source and to the Exchange for our students to read. This process saved money because the student messages were transmitted via The Source after regular business hours when the hourly charges were about half the prime time rates. Unfortunately, the pen pal activity was largely a failure because of the delays in the portage system and the differences in how students in the schools 3,000 miles apart were using the computers. Pen pals did not always have computers available at the same time. Consequently, conversations never really got started between particular students and everyone was frustrated.

The situation radically improved when the activity changed from messages between particular "pals" to short essays between classes. The bombing of Libya was an event that sparked these exchanges. Several of the San Diego students wrote short opinions of this event. The class in New York responded with several of their own opinions and the exchange continued through several turns. This was a successful activity partly because the topic was compelling and one that the 6th graders had strong feelings about. The structure of the exchanges was also easier to manage because the "editorials" were being sent not to individual children but to and from whole classes. The probability of getting a response was much higher and all the children, whether or not they actually wrote an editorial, could feel involved.

Lessons for the Future

There is a clear lesson here for how to use long distance telecommunications. Telecommunications activities over long distances appear to work best when the exchange does not require response of a particular person. This was also reflected in the "guest expert" activity described above in which little was lost if a particular classroom failed to send in any questions. As long as a sufficient number of questions were sent in, the exchanges were valuable to everybody regardless of whether they participated actively or passively; that is, whether they wrote questions or just read the questions and answers that others generated. Highly coordinated activities requiring the response of a particular person at a particular time are best not undertaken between distant schools unless the teachers are willing to work very hard at coordination.

The use of both The Source and the Exchange in our projects illustrates what is probably the most critical principle in using telecommunications as an effective classroom tool. In almost all the activities, students and teachers spent very little time connected to the phone line. Most of the composition of letters and essays was done on word processors. The teachers later transmitted the prepared text files over the phone line keeping the line open a minimum of time. In general, it is best to do all processing as locally as possible. Writing should be done on a word processor. Local messages should be sent via local bulletin boards with expensive commercial services used only for long distance messages that cannot be sent any other way.

In the case of classroom activities that involve searching very large databases, accessing the commercial services may sometimes be unavoidable. But even in this case, many local solutions are possible. Medium size databases can be maintained on a school district computer to which students have free access. Some programs let you quickly get the data you need and then work on it using your own microcomputer. For example, *Weather Machine*, a program by National Geographic Society, lets you call up a computer in Washington D.C. and download to the classroom computer the entire weather service data set for the United States in a matter of seconds. This brief connect time does not add up to a large long distance bill. And once the data is loaded onto the students' floppy disks, the class can use the *Weather Machine* program to display maps of temperature, wind direction, pressure, and more, at any elevation from 0 to 40,000 feet. Once the information is on their own machines, there is, of course, no charge for the time they spend exploring the rich set of data.

Where are We Headed?

A combination of forces are slowly beginning to move telecommunications from the realm of the hobbyist to a more routine part of a teacher's professional toolkit. The hardware is becoming cheaper and more powerful. Bulletin board systems are proliferating and in some cases becoming much easier to use. Some school systems are acquiring local area networks (LANs) to interconnect the microcomputers in a school or computer lab. At the same time, some state education departments are planning and implementing tele-communication systems for administrative and instructional purposes. This combination of individual teachers starting telecommunication activities in their classrooms and districts and states trying to solve larger communication problems may gradually result in integrated communication systems that give many more classrooms access to the outside world.

Local area networks may play an important role in making telecommunications a more routine part of classroom life. LANs provide a communication connection among computers in a school without the use of more expensive phone lines. By connecting one computer in the system to a phone line, any computer in the school is able to communicate with databases and bulletin boards outside the school. The Earth Lab project at Bank Street experimented with integrating local and long distance science activities using a LAN within the school and phone lines to telecommunicate outside the school (Newman 1987, Newman et al. 1989). While a system like Earth Lab may make communication easier and more routine for the individual teachers, it requires a higher level of commitment and expertise on the part of the school or district computer coordinator. As a result, a new profession of communications coordinators may evolve from the grass roots efforts of a few teachers who started with a simple phone line in their classroom.

While the classroom phone line opens up a new world of information and communication, the emphasis should remain on the classroom processes—both the lessons and discussions about the processes involving the classroom computer. The phone line should be used efficiently and sparingly to keep the costs down and not overburden communication resources. A few minutes of "data transmission" a day can keep a class occupied with a variety of communicative activities that spark students' interest by keeping them in contact with the outside world.

References

Glossbrenner, A. (1986). *The Complete Handbook of Personal Computer Communication*. New York: St. Martin's Press.

Levin, J.A., M.M. Riel, R.D. Rowe, and M.J. Boruta. (1985). "Muktuk Meets Jacuzzi: Computer Networks and Elementary School Writers." In *The Acquisition of Written Language: Revision and Response*, edited by S.W. Freedman. Hillsdale, N.J.: Ablex.

McGinnis, M. (1986). "Supporting Science Teachers through Electronic Networking." Paper presented at the New England Educational Research Association, Rockport, Maine.

Newman, D. (1987). "Local and Long Distance Computer Networking for Science Classrooms." *Educational Technology* 1, 6: 20-23.

Newman, D., S.V. Goldman, D. Brienne, I. Jackson, and S. Magzamen. (1989). "Peer Collaboration in Computer-Mediated Science Investigation." *Journal of Educational Computing Research*. 5, 2: 151-166.

Newman, D., and K. Rehfield. (1985). "Using a National Network for Professional Development." Paper presented at the Annual Meetings of the American Educational Research Association, Chicago, Ill.

Quinsaat, M., S. Friel, and R. McCarthy. (1985). "Training Issues in the Teaching of Science, Math, and the Use of Technology. In *Voyage of the **Mimi**:" Perspectives of Teacher Education*, S. Loucks (chair) of the symposium at the Annual Meetings of the American Educational Research Association, Chicago, Ill.

Riel, M.M. (1985). "The Computer Chronicles Newswire: A Functional Learning Environment for Acquiring Literacy Skills." *Journal of Educational Computing Research* 1: 317-337.

10

Science Is Problem Solving

Roy Unruh

To participate in science is to engage in problem solving. To a scientist, problem solving means becoming intellectually interested in phenomena, making observations, developing relationships, and creating models. These relationships and models are then used to predict events and make further observations. These further observations are in turn used to confirm the model, help the scientist modify it, or create an alternative.

Science educators develop materials and teaching strategies that not only help students understand basic concepts in science, but also communicate the nature of science. Students develop an appreciation of science when they can find relationships and create interpretations of events that explain their observations. Technology can assist teachers and students in exploring scientific relationships. Through some of the new software packages, students can develop key problem-solving skills previously learned only in laboratories.

Laboratory Simulations

Science students need to engage in making decisions that cultivate the skills that go with scientific investigation. To this end, some computer programs take advantage of the fact that experiments can be simulated that could not otherwise be conducted.

The IBM *Physics Discovery Series* contains such simulations as investigating the variables that affect the gravitational force on the cabin of a spacecraft, investigating variables that affect the potential and kinetic energy of a roller coaster at an amusement park, and others that use settings that relate physics to high-interest phenomena or are too difficult to reproduce in a laboratory. The educational objectives of these programs include:

- exploring and developing possible interpretations of physical phenomena,
- developing reasoning and problem-solving skills,
- designing experiments to determine how a dependent variable is affected by independent variables, and
- developing scientific models to explain observations.

In the program *Investigating Gravitational Force*, the student commands a spacecraft that has "sensors" that can detect the mass, distance, and density of planets, as well as the gravitational force between the planet and the spacecraft. The student can alter the values of any of the independent variables and then press the "enter" key to see how the gravitational force responds. As this process continues, the student is encouraged to look for patterns or relationships between the gravitational force and the independent variables.

Hrecz (1985) compared how students controlled variables in *Investigating Gravitational Force* with how they scored on controlling variables with the "Bending Rods Piagetian Interview Task" to determine whether or not students can be provided with the same mental encounters in a laboratory simulation program as in the actual laboratory. Students were rated on the basis of the number of variables that were changed in the computer simulation and the verbal responses they made to questions from the interviewer. There was a .78 correlation between student performance of controlling variables with the laboratory interview task. This result suggests that the mental encounters of a student controlling variables with actual laboratory apparatus is highly correlated with the mental process occurring at a computer keyboard for the program used in the study. Thus, laboratory simulation programs can be written to engage the students in higher-level reasoning skills.

Some software programs are designed to simulate alternative models for describing certain physical events. Educational Materials and Equipment Corporation (EME) has a program called *Laws of Motion* that simulates a block sliding down an incline plane. In addition to being able to change variables such as the angle of the incline, the mass of the block, and the friction between the block and plane, the students may select either the Newtonian or the Aristotelian view of falling objects. In either system, the motion of the block may be viewed with graphic comparisons made of the displacement and velocity versus time. Students require such thinking skills as exploring, observing, controlling variables, analyzing data, and evaluating models to complete the task successfully.

While many science educators feel there is no substitute for hands-on laboratory activities, there are several advantages to using the simulation programs. Students can become engaged in the program without teacher supervision. Types of events can be simulated that have a greater student appeal than events that can be simulated in a school laboratory. Questions can be carefully formulated by experts to create the proper background and environment to help students use reasoning skills. And students receive immediate responses to their actions and can learn from their mistakes.

The Nature of Computer Interfacing

Laboratory probes may be inexpensively linked to a computer by way of game ports, printer ports, or circuit cards. These probes can be used to measure temperature, light intensity, force, heat, breathing rate, distance, velocity, and sound. The measurement of these variables can be displayed on the screen in real time as the data are being collected and plotted against time on a graph. This allows the students to see the graphs being generated as the measurements are being taken. This instant display allows the students to explore the effect of changing a variable and immediately note the result.

Since the probes are under the student's control, the student is more likely to see the connection between the measurements from an experiment and the graph of the data and make appropriate interpretations. All of this can be accomplished without the drudgery and time-consuming effort of plotting data points before conclusions can be reached. With such a large investment of time in collecting and graphing data, students lose interest in exploring the effect of other variables and feel they are penalized for their curiosity. With these probes, students can spend more time encountering and cultivating problem-solving skills.

One of the most common probes is a temperature probe. The software typically allows the student to either display the numerical values of the temperature or to plot temperature taken at selected time intervals. Students may explore the frequently misunderstood concepts of heat and temperature by comparing the effect of adding a small amount of hot water with that of adding a larger amount of warm water to a given container of water. As the probes are placed in different environments, students will note the changes in temperature from the graphs as well as the rates at which the temperatures change by observing the slopes of the graphs. Students may be given a graph of changing temperatures and asked to change the temperature of the probe to match the given temperature graph. These experiences are excellent for relating events with graphical representation and interpreting data.

Students may take advantage of multiple temperature probes in experiments involving the performance of cardboard box greenhouses. One probe may be used to monitor the temperature of water cans used for heat storage inside the greenhouse while another records the outside temperature. This experiment can run for 24 hours, with the data recorded on a disk and then displayed for analysis during the class. The effect of energy placed in storage can be shown on the night-time temperature. Several variables can be changed, including the size of the collected surface, the volume of the greenhouse, and the amount of water used for storage. This experiment demonstrates another useful aspect of the computer: It can collect data over long periods of time without the presence of the experimenter.

Motion Detector

A motion detector was developed by the Technical Education Research Center (TERC; Barclay 1986) from a sonic transducer used in Polaroid cameras. The motion probe sends out short pulses of high-frequency sound and then measures the time required for the echo to return to the unit. With this information, the program can calculate and graphically display the position, velocity, and acceleration of an object from 0.5 meters to 8 meters from the probe. The data and any of the graphs may be displayed as the motion is monitored. Various types of motion may be investigated, including the motion of individual students, toys, a pendulum, or a falling body. Data can then be analyzed, transformed, printed, and saved on disks.

From a position-versus-time graph of the motion, questions can be asked of students to direct their understanding of displacement, velocity, and acceleration. Students might be asked where on the position-versus-time graph they turned around and approached the transducer, if they ever moved at constant velocity, where they moved the fastest, what their speed was at a particular time, and so on. After students have been shown either a position-versus-time graph or a speed-versus-time graph, they can move so as to duplicate the graph.

The motion detector has been used with different students, ranging from 6th graders to humanities students taking physics at the college level. In both groups, motion was introduced by observing graphs created by the movement of their own bodies. The 6th graders developed a sophisticated understanding of motion and of position and velocity graphs. The college humanities students also showed excellent achievement, nearly equaling the performance of freshman physics majors on similar test questions.

Measurements of Human Body Functions

To make measurements and conduct experiments involving the human body provides strong motivation and interest for most students. Light-sensitive probes have been used by several manufacturers to measure the change in light transmission through thin layers of skin caused by variations of blood flow or pulse rate. In school, students can measure the pulses of class members and note differences and similarities. Hypotheses that may account for these differences, as well as what may cause a change in the pulse rate of individual students, can be generated. Variables such as amount of exercise before a measurement is taken, physical conditioning, and the effect of caffeine can all be tested in the classroom.

* * *

The educational community has placed increasing emphasis on developing thinking and reasoning skills in this decade. The National Science Board has stressed the importance of learning the skills used in observing, classifying, communicating, measuring, hypothesizing, inferring, designing investigations and experiments, collecting data, drawing conclusions, and making generalizations. Acquiring these thinking and problem-solving skills can surely be enhanced by using the computer in high-quality laboratory simulations by using software that allows students to associate the unfolding of a graph with the transpiring of an event.

11

Computers and Writing: The Inevitable Social Context

Andee Rubin

*W*hat would you do if you were a 14-year-old girl living in a tiny, inaccessible rural village and you felt your world was uncomfortably limited? What if, to make matters worse, you didn't like a single one of the available boys? Some of the solutions that come to mind involve written language: reading about other places and people to expand your knowledge about the rest of the world, or trying to find male pen pals to establish contact with some other (hopefully more suitable) young men. Several teenage girls in McGrath, Alaska, a town of 500, took exactly this approach. Presented with the opportunity to use an electronic mail system, they composed the following "open letter" to potential suitors:

Calling All Men

Hi,

This note is to all you good-looking guys out there in the world. There are two of us writing so we'll tell you a little bit about ourselves. Our names are Sally Foster and Terry James. We're both 14 and stuck in a small town in Alaska, called McGrath. We have a pretty big problem and we hope that you guys will help us out. We have a short supply of foxy dudes here. So if you are a total fine babe PLEASE write us!!

Write: (their address) and hurry!   Keywords: *McGrath, Male Order Men*

Not to be outdone, two girls in Holy Cross, an even smaller town, composed their own message. They tried hard to outshine their rivals and be even more attractive to the boys. In particular, they targeted their audience by addressing their message to "Juneau boys." They also spent a long and fairly tedious half-hour mastering the intricacies of the word processor in order to produce the heart at the end of their note:

Good Looking Juneau Boys

Our names are Josie Adams and Evelyn Fields. We like skiing, basketball, hockey, writing letters to cute boys, and we would be more than pleased if any of you cute boys would write to us. We don't have any boyfriends. So you don't have to worry about that! We also would like you to send a picture when you write. (You are going to write, aren't you?) We will send you a picture, too. Joyce is 14, and Elaine is 13. Well, please write soon! We are waiting for your letters!!!

```
        xxx  xxx
      xxxxxx  xxxxxx
   xxxxxxxxxxxxxxxxxxxx
     xxxxxxxxxxxxxxxxx
      xxxxxxxxxxxxxx
       xxxxxxxxxxx
         xxxxx
          xx
```

WE SEND YOU OUR HEARTS!

SINCERELY, JOSIE AND EVELYN

Keywords: *Juneau Boys, Holy Cross Girls*

These two examples illustrate one intimate connection between social interaction and writing: the social environment as a source of purpose and audience for written communication. Without a reason to communicate, these students would not have written as they did; without their perception of the importance of that reason, they would not have persevered in their exploration of the word processor. The embedding of the writing task in a social context created a powerful educational opportunity for them.

The common vision of educational software stands in stark contrast to this scenario: students working alone at individual terminals, receiving much of their evaluation and feedback from the computer, working on a series of tasks determined by the computer. The letters above are the product of a different approach to educational technology, one in which the students control the computer to achieve their own social and educational goals. This chapter describes software that unites the computer and the social environment into a powerful educational environment in which students can improve their writing in several important ways (Bruce, Michaels, and Watson 1985; Rubin and Bruce 1985, 1986).

Computers as Cognitive and Social Tools

What is the computer's unique contribution to this educational context? First, and most frequently mentioned, is the computer's role as a tool. Word processors reduce the pain of editing and revision, allowing students to format their work, produce professional-looking copies of text, and easily read their own and other's pieces by eliminating problems of illegibility.

Spelling checkers help students make their final drafts more readable, and on-line thesauruses provide resources for students searching for more precise words. Some schools have also begun to use outline processors, programs that allow students to compose and manipulate an outline before and during writing. In the future, there will, undoubtedly, be more sophisticated writing tools readily available to students: on-line dictionaries, multimedia dictionaries, and complete grammar checkers. These tools all facilitate the cognitive aspects of writing, but, especially because writing involves both a writer and a *reader*, the computer's effect on the social context is equally important. Of course, there is a social context surrounding any activity in school, and using computers for writing is no exception.

The assignment the teacher has given to the class, the physical space in which the students work, the amount of time they spend talking to one another and the teacher about the piece, the choice of audience, and the purpose students have for writing all influence how writing tools are used and what students learn. But it turns out that computers, in addition to being writing tools, can themselves create and modify social environments. This is especially true for a subject such as writing, in which the social environment is central to both the learning process and the subject matter. What follows is a description of a software package designed with the social context of writing in mind.

Quill

Quill was designed by Bolt, Beranek, Newman Inc., and the NETWORK Inc. to help students learn to write. It includes both writing tools and writing environments; that is, it attempts to affect both the cognitive and social environments in which students write. Interestingly, classroom experiences with *Quill* demonstrated that the social environment in the classroom changed in ways the developers never anticipated. In fact, the complexity of the interaction among software, curriculum, teacher, students, and administration was one of the significant aspects of the field test. The following descriptions demonstrate how important it is to consider the social context when using technology in schools. Even though *Quill* is no longer commercially available (it was marketed by D.C. Heath from 1983 to 1985), the perspective it embodied has found its way into other pieces of software; thus, the following descriptions are as important as ever for conceptualizing the interaction between writing software and the social context of the classroom.

Quill consists of four programs -- *Planner*, *Library*, *Mailbag*, and *Writer's Assistant*. *Planner* is a tool that helps students become more organized and efficient in their writing. *Library* and *Mailbag* provide the social environment options, allowing for different audiences, purposes, and genres for writing. *Writer's Assistant* is a general word processor and contains all the standard word processing capabilities (e.g., add, delete, replace, and search), as well as a unique facility for reformatting a paragraph of text into individual sentences so that errors of capitalization, punctuation, and structure are more visible.

Planner

Planner was designed to help students (1) generate and organize ideas for their writing and (2) reflect on their writing as it takes shape. A planner consists of a series of questions or prompts that encourage students to brainstorm, organize, or revise their pieces.

Because students can create and modify planners, they can be shared and edited just like any other piece of writing. To use *Planner* as an idea-generating device, a teacher might involve students in a brainstorming session to generate a list of questions or topics to consider for an assignment. If they are writing movie reviews, the students might consider acting quality, photography, intended audience, or subject. The teacher can make this list into a planner on the computer so that when students begin composing their movie reviews, they can generate ideas.

At the end of a writing assignment, *Planner* helps students review their work. It might ask students to identify a possible weak point in their piece or to think of another example they might include. Using a revision planner, students can rework a written draft. For example, Steve and Karen are going to write a review of their favorite restaurant, Chuck's Parlor. Using their class-generated Planner for restaurant reviews, they type in responses to most of the topic questions: overall assessment, best food, price, atmosphere, location, hours, needed improvements, and appropriate patrons. After printing their notes on the printer, they decide how best to organize what they want to say, composing sentences and paragraphs from their notes.

Across the room, Melinda and Jose are working on a movie review. They decide to modify Steve and Karen's restaurant review planner, since they feel some of it is relevant to their piece. They keep the questions on overall assessment, appropriate patrons, and needed improvements but substitute other questions that are more useful for their purpose. They then post a note on the electronic bulletin board using *Mailbag*, telling everyone that they have constructed a movie review planner, in case someone else would also like to use it.

Thus, even in this cognitively oriented tool, students are working in a software-facilitated social environment in which they can share writing resources. The two writing environments of *Quill—Library* and *Mailbag*—focus even more on this aspect of the classroom.

Library

Library creates an environment that enables students and teachers to share information and compositions. Students and teachers can write about topics they choose and store their writing in *Library* so it is available to other computer users. Pieces of writing are organized by author(s), title, and topic (identified by one or more keywords), just as in a "real" library. Thus, *Library* performs three major functions:

- It creates a communication environment in which students are encouraged to write for their peers as well as for the teacher.
- It organizes writing in different ways.
- It provides easy access to stored pieces of writing.

Library encourages writing, facilitates sharing, and eases the teacher's record-keeping burden. The following examples demonstrate how *Library* influences the social structure in a classroom.

A teacher wants to help students develop skills in giving instructions. She decides that each student will contribute an article to a class "How-to-Do-It Manual." Leah wants to write some instructions for building a bird feeder and add it to *Library*. She uses the *Quill Library* disk that contains other "How-to-Do-It" articles. She adds an entry to this disk, which already contains five articles by other students in the class. When she finishes her article, Leah types her title, "How to Build a Bird Feeder to Attract Birds," followed by her name.

The program then asks for one or more keywords that will give others a good idea of what her article is about. Leah looks at the list of existing keywords generated by students who have already entered their articles. She types in the word "carpentry." The program automatically updates the keyword list, so carpentry will appear the next time anyone uses this disk, either to add an article or to read the articles other students have written. Her article thus becomes part of the "How-to-Do-It Manuals," automatically indexed for quick reference.

Later, Arnold tells Leah he has read her article and couldn't follow one of the instructions. After she explains it to him, he suggests a way she might make her piece more understandable. Together, they rework the paragraph in question, and save the new version. Arnold then has the opportunity to add his name as a second author of the piece and, with Leah's permission, he does so. Other students will see both authors' names when they list the articles on this disk.

Library provides a particular social environment for students' writing, one in which sharing, evaluating, reading, and editing one's own and other people's writing is united in a communicative framework. The structure of *Library* — just as in a real library — promotes sharing because each composition is indexed in ways that invite access. Also, students, in adding their writing to *Library*, confront the need to make their writing available, since they must choose keywords by which their pieces can be accessed. Students using *Quill* often respond to this need by making one of their five allowed keywords "advertise" their piece, using eye-catching words such as "loony" along with a few serious keywords. This is only one of the ways in which students demonstrated their often-quiescent knowledge of communication strategies.

Mailbag

Mailbag allows for direct communication among individual students, groups of students, and teachers. It combines features of the post office, the telephone, and a bulletin board in that written messages can be sent between individuals or a message can be posted for a group. *Mailbag* enhances instruction by:

- enhancing written communication to varying, but specific, audiences (for example, friends and classmates),
- allowing different kinds of writing to occur (for example, informing, persuading, instructing, entertaining), and
- motivating students to write more by personalizing the experience.

Mailbag has two complementary functions. First, students can send messages. In a classroom with an active mailbag, Jacqueline sends a message to Marilyn about a very embarrassing experience at the movies on Saturday. Matt sends a message to the Animal Club asking for membership information. Jon, who has an oral history assignment and wants to interview some senior citizens about their early school experiences, uses the Bulletin Board part of *Mailbag* to ask the class if any of their grandparents were born in town. In each of these cases, *Mailbag* is an efficient vehicle for sharing and seeking information, while providing opportunities for written expression that often are not present in school.

Mailbag's second function is to receive messages. In that same classroom, each student checks his or her mail. They can also request mail from specific groups to which they belong. Finally, they can view the Bulletin Board and read messages that have been posted for everyone. For example, Maria consults *Mailbag* by typing her name. She has two messages, one titled "Urgent" and the other "Secret Letter." She reads both and learns that her mother has left her lunch money at the office (a message conveniently left for her by the teacher), and that her ardent, but as yet unidentified admirer, wants to meet her after school. When she asks for messages for the Soccer Club, she finds out that there is a practice on Thursday after school. Consulting the Bulletin Board, she learns that Wallie is looking for recommendations for a new adventure book to read and is soliciting opinions for and against each suggested book.

The Social Context Revisited

Our experiences demonstrate that software like *Quill* could influence the social context of a classroom to encourage real communication, by helping students focus on audience and purpose, revise with clear reasons, and develop a literate community. Of course, the teacher plays a large and critical role in determining the characteristics of the interactions that evolve. Some teachers used software and accompanying suggestions in the teacher's guide as a starting point for enriching writing instruction in their classrooms in ways that went far beyond the software, including a book of love stories to inanimate objects (inspired when the teacher confided to his class that he loved his bright red sneakers), a series on TV plays written by a group of four 6th grade girls, a community calendar decorated with pictures and student poetry and containing the birthdays of all 50 village residents, and several monthly classroom newspapers.

The most interesting results, however, were the unanticipated interactions among the computer, the software, and the classroom. In one classroom, a series of events led to a 6th grade girl's discovery that there are often real and important reasons for revision. The entire class had attended a schoolwide Black History Show in the auditorium and when they returned, the teacher announced an optional assignment: write a review of the show. Those who chose to write could use *Quill* to produce a final version of their review. Students got access to the computer in the order in which they finished their drafts. One girl, Margaret, included the following paragraph in the first draft of her revision:

"The scenery was pretty good, and the light was bright enough, but the sound was not good. Mr. Hodges was speaking very loudly and was good on the stage. I think the show deserves three stars because it was very good."

While Margaret was standing in line to use the computer, her friend, Mary, finished a draft and joined her. Margaret read Mary's rather negative review, which contained the following paragraph: "I don't know what happened to the Glee Club, they were almost all weak. The audience couldn't hear them. They sounded soft then they went loud. It was a disaster!"

When Margaret had her turn at the computer, she made several changes in her review. Some were minor, but there was one major change. In the middle of the paragraph included above, she inserted several new sentences. The piece then read: "The scenery wasn't much, and the light was kind of dull, and the sound wasn't very good. Mr. Hodges was speaking loud and clearly, and he was good on the stage. When the Glee Club was singing so nice, Mary got very jealous and asked Mrs. Evans to be in the Glee Club. But when Mrs. Evans said 'no,' she wrote bad things about the Glee Club on the computer upstairs."

Margaret had made a quite substantial revision in her review. It was not motivated by a teacher's telling her that revision is an important part of effective writing, but by her sense that her audience (the class) would want an explanation of the discrepancies between her review and Mary's. This is the very essence of good writing: the incorporation of critical reading and audience awareness into the writing process. The contributions to this powerful lesson for Margaret were many—the computer that created the need for a queue in which she read her classmate's piece, the teacher, and the social context all contributed in important ways. It is this interaction that should be at the center of future software design and research into technology's place in education and the use of computers in schools.

References

Anderson, J.R., C.F. Boyle, and B.J. Reiser. (April 1985). "Intelligent Tutoring Systems." *Science* 228, 456-462.

Brown, J.S., and R.R. Burton. "Diagnostic Models for Procedural Bugs in Basic Mathematical Skills." *Cognitive Science* 2.

Bruce, C., S. Michaels, and K. Watson-GIGO. (Feb. 1985). "How Computers Can Change the Writing Process." *Language Arts*.

Bruce, B., A. Rubin, and C. Barnhardt. (In press). *Electronic Quills*. Hillsdale, N.J.: Lawrence Erlbaum.

Clancey, W.J. (1982). "Tutoring Rules for Guiding a Case Method Dialogue." In *Intelligent Tutoring Systems*, edited by D. Sleeman and J.S. Brown. New York: Academic Press, Inc.

Frase, L.T. (1983). "The Unix Writer's Workbench Software: Philosophy." *The Bell System Technical Journal*. 62, 6: 1883-1980.

O'Shea, T., and J. Self. (1983). *Learning and Teaching with Computers: Artificial Intelligence in Education*. Brighton, England: The Harvester Press.

Rubin, A.D., and B.C. Bruce. (1986). "Learning with **Quill**: Lessons for Students, Teachers, and Software Designers." In *Contexts of School-based Literacy*, edited by T. Raphael. New York: Random House.

Rubin, A.D., B.C. Bruce, and the **Quill** project. (1985). "**Quill**: Reading and Writing with a Microcomputer." In *Advances in Reading and Language Research*, edited by B.A. Hutson. Greenwich, Conn.: JAI Press.

Sleeman, D. (1982). "Assessing Aspects of Competence in Basic Algebra." In *Intelligent Tutoring Systems*, edited by D. Sleeman and J.S. Brown. New York: Academic Press, Inc.

Soloway, E., K. Ehrlich, J. Bonar, and J. Greenspan. (1982). *What Do Novices Know about Programming?* Norwood, N.J.: Abex.

White, B.Y., and J.R. Frederiksen. (1986). "Intelligent Tutoring Systems Based Upon Qualitative Model Evolutions." Proceedings of the Fifth National Conference on Artificial Intelligence, Philadelphia, Pa.

12

A Personal Account of Computer Use and Humanities Teaching

Benjamin H. Thomas

*W*hen we look at computer use in humanities and social science curriculums, there is great potential for impact on student learning should stand-alone personal computers become commonplace in classrooms. Although computer-assisted instruction has impacted education, tool software and the application of standard software such as word processing packages, database management programs, and spreadsheets can have a far greater impact on humanities teaching. From computers come new and intriguing variations of what teachers have always done — make students think, see connections, and ask questions.

Word Processing Software in the Classroom

For humanities classrooms, word processing software is the most obviously useful tool. A significant number of students are already using word processors for writing assignments, tests, reports, and letters. Teachers, too, are already using word processors — saving their work on a disk for easy revision next time the unit is taught, making notes on the assignment after the unit is completed, and varying their basic message according to which student is to receive it. The magic of a word processor is, of course, ease and cleanliness of revision; teachers and students love it, and better papers result.

The application and use of the word processing software can be expanded beyond the typical scenario. What follows is an account of a unit that I prepared and taught to four classes of 7th and 8th graders at the Sidwell Friends School, an independent Quaker school in Washington, D.C. My primary unit objective was to use a word processor in teaching the writing of poetry.

Working with Sally Selby and her four classes of vertically grouped 7th and 8th graders, I developed an approach to teaching poetry that I hoped would encourage the students to see their poetry as more of a process than a product; one that would produce poets as much as poetry. It is the experience of many teachers that students are fiercely protective of their own writing, especially poetry; that the rough draft and the final are the same; and that revision is punishment. Here is where the word processor came in. It was our hope, supported by the experience of others who had worked with students in their writing, that the ease and neatness of the revising process would encourage students to revise their work more readily.

We began by examining several poems by recognized authors —poems that had been entered into the computer. Viewing poetry on a monitor was in part little different from using a "hard" paper copy. First, we looked at all the proper things — images, alliteration, rhythm. But we studied word selection by generating a list of synonyms for a critical word in one of the poems and then inserting a synonym into the poem on the screen. Of all the efforts to look at the "real" poems, this was the most successful—students started to see the power of the right word in the right place.

We had asked students to write their own poems and read these exercises aloud in class. Each day I put some of their poems up on the monitor's screen for discussion. We looked at what worked and what did not, according to the intent of the student. I had read an article in the *Washington Post* in the fall of 1985 about the use of ThinkTank in meetings, which suggested that participants in a meeting where the focus was on a screen (in that case, one that showed the organizing program) were notably cooperative and made relevant contributions. With that in mind, I hoped that the competitive element always present in classrooms would be dampened by the presence of the monitor. And, in fact, there were few pejorative comments about the poems that came up on the screen. Though students often suggested changes in another's poem, they did so without saying or implying that their way was better.

As a final assignment for the unit, we asked each student to produce his or her best poem. Students' rough drafts went into the computer as soon as they came in, sometimes typed in by me, sometimes by the students themselves. Interestingly, few students wanted to play with the machine; and even fewer really knew how to use it. This was the beginning of a process that continued for several days. I would sit with students at the computer and we would discuss their poems, what they liked and disliked, and what I liked and disliked.

Some of the changes were explored on the spot, but often I would ask them to go home and work on one line or section overnight, and come in with revisions the next day.

The success of this process varied from student to student. There were many who sought me out eagerly before school or during free time to get their changes onto the screen. While I worked with individuals, other students worked on their poetry in pairs, by themselves, or with the other teacher. A colleague commenting on the process said that when she was in school she had never been given the sense that revision was part of the writing process. She also noted that the way in which the teacher and student worked together at the computer created an entirely new relationship, and that she had never seen any of her teachers as resources to the extent that this process mandates.

At the end of this process, when all students had a poem entered and revised on the disk, we printed them out and copied them so that each student had an anthology of student poetry. This is another common and valuable use of a word processing package: compiling and producing collections of student writing.

Students did not endorse the use of the computer wholeheartedly. A few (perhaps one out of four) expressed initial revulsion at the mix of poetry and computers — of soulful art and soulless machines — and that attitude had not entirely left at the end of the unit. For myself, writing poetry seemed as easy on the computer as by hand. I was much more ready to revise it and I found myself experimenting to a much greater degree than I would have done under ordinary circumstances. It may be worth pointing out, however, that only one student did the first draft on a computer (at home) and that what we were about was revision rather than writing. That aspect of the process was clearly successful. Ms. Selby, who had done little work with computers before, agreed with me that the students' work was significantly better as a result of the extensive revising.

There are a number of additional ways to use a personal computer in this unit. We did nothing with random generation of poetry, for example, nor did we track any of the students' work with the personal computer, but the essential task of getting students to write and revise poetry was successful. I would do it again and I believe that Ms. Selby would do it again also. I hope that this kind of computer use will spread to other classrooms in the school.

Spreadsheets and Databases in Social Studies

Use of other standard software tools, such as spreadsheets and database management programs, is far behind that of word processing, but these uses hold potential for exciting changes in teaching. The cause-and-effect relationship and the "what-if" kind of thinking that they generate is critical in a social studies curriculum. In another experimental unit, I worked on database building in social studies.

The topic of the unit was "social stratification." I joined a class of 8th graders after the students had read a chapter on that subject in their sociology text. With Alan Braun, their regular social studies teacher, and me in the classroom for the rest of the unit, the students read *Working* by Studs Terkel, with each student specifically responsible for relating approximately 10 of the 133 interviews in the book to what they learned from the sociology text.

In the first class, I explained what a database was, comparing it to the expertise that a doctor builds up by training and practice, with each experience being a file in the doctor's database. I connected it to the unit by explaining that we would look at the interviews in *Working* and combine what each of the individuals had to say about their job to build a picture of what the book as a whole said.

After a week of general discussion about the book, we developed questions about the interviews to be answered by each student. The questions were predominantly factual (sex, approximate age, race, if known), but many of them called for students to make judgments (e.g., how the subject liked the job on a scale of one to five, what their motivations were for taking the job). We added numerical prestige ratings from a survey done in 1980 and the Equal Employment Opportunity Commission job-classification rating. Students readily accepted that all their responses had to be numerical or multiple choice in form.

All interview data were entered into the computer, and when the database was complete, we looked at the results. Students could ask to see the correlation between answers to any pairs of questions, or to see what one discrete group said as contrasted with the entire set of interviewees. For example, the workers in the highest stanine of prestige did not have a correspondingly high level of job satisfaction; women and individuals holding minority status tended to share negative attitudes about their jobs. Other similar results were equally thought provoking for the students.

The students clearly believed that entering their own opinions into the database mattered a great deal. During assignments, students looked at connections, tried out hypotheses, and thought analytically and creatively—all key skills for social studies instruction.

*   *   *

The preceding curriculum units exemplify my individual style and philosophy of teaching, but computers adapt with ease to any approach. My teaching has been enhanced by computer use, and, while I know that using computers has changed my teaching, I am equally sure that I have not been pushed where I did not want to go.

Teachers are pioneers in developing how best to use computers in the humanities. As we develop new uses, we will feel the discomfort that accompanies change, but we can delight in what lies ahead.

13

"Storylords": Decisions in the Creation of an Instructional Television Series

Thomas DeRose
Martha Deming

Norbert:	Who are you?
Lexor:	I am Lexor, Storylord of Mojuste. And you?
Norbert:	I'm Norbert. . . .boy of Wisconsin.
Lexor:	Norbert, there is no time to lose. The wicked Storylord, Thorzuul, seeks to conquer my planet. Then he will attack yours! I am old—my time in this body is short. I need an Apprentice Storylord to help defeat Thorzuul and save both our planets. Will you accept the challenge?
Norbert:	Well. . . .sure, I . . . .But I have to be home by dinner time.

So begin the adventures of Norbert in the instructional television series "Storylords," which introduces 2nd through 4th grade students to reading comprehension skills.

In the case of "Storylords," research in Wisconsin indicated a need for a reading series for the lower primary grades. Consultations with reading experts established that the series should present a set of reading and comprehension strategies that an accomplished reader would apply—strategies such as activating prior knowledge before starting to read, making inferences by combining what you know with what is on the page, defining an unknown word through its context, and so on. These consultations led to the creation of a project team consisting of reading experts, a production crew, and writers who combined their skills to produce such a series.

In designing and developing "Storylords," we considered the content to be presented, the intended audience, and the series' goals and objectives—all of which are examined in greater depth later in this chapter.

Children in grades two through four were the selected audience for the series. The selection of story line was based on its potential for this age group: To defeat Thorzuul and save the citizens of the planet Mojuste, Norbert must learn and apply reading comprehension strategies to the problems Thorzuul poses. Additionally, the childrens' level of cognitive development was considered in determining the balance between the amount of information presented and the pace of presentation.

Television as an Instructional Medium

The power *and* limitations of television dictate to a large degree what can be done in an instructional television series. Television is good at holding and focusing attention, systematically presenting ideas, and maximizing the efficiency of presentation. On the other hand, television is basically unidirectional (i.e, noninteractive); it must satisfy the least competent viewer; and it is largely limited to presenting abstract ideas through concrete examples. Instructional television users normally prefer that programs be limited to about 15 minutes of viewing time. This limitation of 15 minutes is preferred for two reasons: to limit the total amount of information presented in one session, and to allow for pre- and post-viewing activities within a normal block of instructional time (50 minutes).

We cannot expect children who watch instructional television to be able to perform all tasks presented in the program simply by viewing the program. Television generally is not the best medium to accomplish changes in performance. Therefore, teachers must use the medium to support, not accomplish, their learning goals. Television can and should present a concept (as in "Storylord," a reading strategy) in such a way that students are able to *under-stand* and *appreciate* its use. Following the televised illustration, the teacher can show the student how to apply the strategy.

An exception to this general rule might be an instance in which an instructional television program presents a limited amount of information, such as what the letter "A" looks and sounds like. We are all familiar with the great success of "Sesame Street" in demonstrating that such basic skills can be taught through television. However, the learning of more complex conceptual knowledge within a 15-minute period cannot be accomplished, certainly not in any measurable way.

What, then, should be expected from a 15-minute instructional television presentation? The answer to this question has a tremendous impact on the design of a program.

Program Design

Perhaps the best way to describe what can be expected is through an analogy shared by Leonard Waks during a Science Technology and Society meeting at Penn State University where the use of televisions was being discussed (personal communication 1986). In a typical trigonometry class, a teacher may prove a theorem at the board. The hope is that the students will understand the proof. The teacher might expect a student to say: "Oh yeah, I get it!" However, the teacher would not expect the student to then be able to perform the proof. This ability would come only after repeated attempts and much practice. Nevertheless, though the teacher would be unable to measure the student's understanding of the proof, he or she would feel comfortable knowing that the student "got it."

Applying this analogy to instructional television, we can expect that after viewing a program students will be able to state that they understand the message. Perhaps they will be able to explain how they came to understand the message—what elements of the program made it understandable to them. In most cases, however, they will not be able to demonstrate an ability to perform according to the message.

In the case of "Storylords," after viewing the video program that introduces the strategy of identifying the elements of a story, students may say, "Yes, I understand it." Students may be able to explain what they understand. A story must have six parts: setting, characters, problem, goal, episodes, and resolution. Without these, it is not a story. They may be able to say why this is important to know ("Knowing story structure helps one understand a story") and even why they think this is so ("When Mandy had to solve the problem, she used what she knew about story structure to do it"). However, if asked to identify the elements of a story and to show how this helps to understand the story better, the students would probably fail. This ability will come only after students work with stories under the guidance of a teacher.

A 15-minute instructional television program, then, can create understanding in the audience without necessarily bringing about measurable changes in behavior.

The Content: Reading-Comprehension Strategies

"Storylords" was developed by Wisconsin Public Television Networks (1985) to improve reading comprehension and reading comprehension instruction in grades two through four. Research (Duffy, Roehler, and Mason 1984) identified comprehension strategies employed by competent readers, some of which are already taught in regular reading instruction (e.g., identifying a main idea and supporting details) and some of which have traditionally been left untaught (e.g., improving understanding by connecting what you already know with what you are reading). A skilled reader learns this set of strategies and applies them where appropriate. If the strategies can be taught to and used by young readers, their ability to comprehend what they read should improve.

The goal of "Storylords" is to present comprehension strategies in such a way that students adopt them and incorporate them into their regular processes of reading comprehension.

Thinking about Thinking. Reading can be thought of as a process in which the reader continually experiences new problems to solve: determining who the main character is; understanding a new, unrecognizable word; and finding answers to questions. To solve a problem, the reader must be able to recognize and identify it as a specific problem, decide on the appropriate solution, apply the strategy, consider the success of the application, and reassess any or all of these steps as necessary. For example, Norbert is trying to learn to throw a spiral pass by following the directions in a booklet. He is able to understand the words, but does not know enough about throwing a football to understand the directions. In science class the next day, Norbert learns a special strategy for reading assignments that do not make sense: stop, think, reread, ask, read over. In the application of this strategy to the football booklet, Norbert has identified a problem—he cannot make sense of what he is reading even though he understands the words. He knows that he needs additional information in order to figure out how to throw a spiral so he applies the strategy—he stops reading, thinks about his problem, rereads the text, decides that he needs help from someone who knows how to throw a spiral, gets that help, and then re-read the text to get the information he wanted from the booklet in the first place.

Such introspective problem solving and strategic behavior requires readers to reflect on their mental processes. Metacognition, as this process is called, poses problems for 2nd and 3rd grade children. Young children do not understand what to do when directed to think about their thinking processes. They cannot *consciously* pause and consider their own thinking. This ability develops later.

The Audience

Children in grades 2 through 4 are quite competent at observing and copying the behavior of others. Certainly this modeling behavior is a significant part of human development. In fact, the research into the effects on children of violence and other antisocial behavior seen on television shows that children do model the behavior they see (Gadow and Spratkin 1989, Huesmann and Malamuth 1986, Singer 1989).

Our task, therefore, was to create situations in which characters would find themselves in a problem situation that would require the application of the appropriate strategy. To facilitate the modeling, the situation would have to be identified by the audiences as desirable or attractive—one in which viewers could imagine themselves.

Getting Audience Attention Through Fantasy. We wanted to create a situation in which reading problems would have tangible consequences, as well as a situation to which the audience could relate. Certainly, today's children have a good deal of experience with, and are very fond of, fantasy action adventures. Therefore, this genre is effective with young children as a motivational tool.

Briefly, "Storylords'" plot is this: An evil wizard, Thorzuul, is attempting to gain control of the planet Mojuste by finding those who cannot read well and turning them to stone. The good Storylord, Lexor, enlists the aid of Norbert, an average boy. Whenever someone is stuck on a reading problem posed by Thorzuul, Norbert is summoned to Mojuste, where he must determine the problem and use a reading strategy to solve it. Such a context creates a situation where the problem is significant and warrants the attention of Norbert and the audience.

Grounding in Real Life

The next development task was to determine how to provide Norbert with appropriate strategies to solve the problems and thwart Thorzuul. Perhaps, like

Norbert, many children judge the usefulness of school by the relevance school has for them. Therefore, it is appropriate that Norbert acquires the information he needs from his teacher, Mrs. Framish, and from classroom reading instruction. This approach helps the audience see and appreciate the value of education for solving problems that are important to them.

While the situations in which Norbert finds himself on Mojuste capture attention, they are not a part of the audience's daily life. To show the audience how these strategies relate to daily life, each program also contains a problem that is a part of Norbert's everyday "earthly" life and is solved by the application of the same strategy used to solve the problem on Mojuste.

Decisions about Characters

It was important that Norbert's character be someone with whom the audience could identify. Norbert is not perfect. He is a little overweight and a little "frumpy." While interested in sports, he does not excel in them. He likes to learn but is not enthusiastic about school.

So that there could be an exchange of dialogue with Norbert, he was given a friend, Jason, who is a little more practical, not as prone to fantasy. Perhaps that is why Lexor chose Norbert, not Jason, to be his apprentice.

Field testing while the series was under production indicated a potential problem: both principal characters were boys. If the situations being created were ones that boys would be more likely to experience, girls in the audience might have difficulty identifying with the situations. This finding prompted the creation of Norbert's sister, Mandy, who is a year or so younger than Norbert. While Norbert often provides guidance for Mandy in reading comprehension skills, Mandy has abilities of her own. She can, for example, throw a football with a perfect spiral. And when introduced by Norbert to reading strategies, she demonstrates her adeptness at quickly grasping and applying them in practical situations.

In fact, Mandy accompanies Norbert on trips to Mojuste and, in several instances, thwarts Thorzuul completely on her own.

The Artistic Element

While developers and producers of the series were knowledgeable about child development and reading comprehension, they also had experience with what captures the attention of children and what makes good television. Art had as much to do with the development of the series as did science.

Science and art combined, for example, in the selection of the actor who played Norbert. The character not only fit the instructional needs of the series but also "looked right" and was easy to direct. Artistic elements used to capture the attention of the audience and make them *enjoy* watching include special effects (Norbert's space travel machine), costumes (Thorzuul's broad-shouldered cape), props (Storylord gloves), music (Thorzuul's entry theme), and comedy (Thorzuul's sidekick, Milkbreath).

Evaluation

Television is an artistic medium; ignoring this fact in the development of instructional television can limit both its effectiveness and its appeal. Ultimately, the success of "Storylords" will be determined by how well the series blends science and art, as well as by the way it is used in the classroom.

Field Testing

Evaluation of "Storylords" was conducted in several stages. As previously mentioned, a preliminary version was field tested. During production of the series, evaluations were conducted at points where modifications to content outlines, program treatment, and elements could be made (Wilsman 1984). Teachers, reading supervisors, principals, and students evaluated the scripts and content outlines as they were developed. In addition, observations and interviews were conducted in classrooms to determine the ways reading was taught so that the necessary assistance could be provided through the accompanying teacher guide or inservice training. Observations also were made about the extent to which students and teachers referred to, and used, reading comprehension presented in "Storylords."

Based on the recommendations of the evaluators, the scripts and content outlines were revised. For example, the character Lexor, the good storylord, was strengthened to match that of Thorzuul, the wicked storylord, who was found to be very appealing to students.

Students found the "Storylords" programs highly appealing and applauded after viewing them. Boys sat on the edges of their seats and volunteered equally as often as girls to answer questions about the storyline of the program and the strategy. After the lessons, students were able to state the reading strategies in their own words. During the week following each lesson, students referred to the program's characters and reading strategies. All students were anxious to see the next program.

Final Evaluation

After the series was complete, we conducted an extensive evaluation to determine the effectiveness of "Storylords" with 2nd, 3rd, and 4th grade students (Wilsman 1987). In addition to student and teacher interviews, standardized tests in vocabulary and comprehension were administered to students in the fall and spring of 1985 and 1986. Results showed substantial increases in mean comprehension and vocabulary scores for students who had participated in the "Storylords" program. Improvements in comprehension were greatest at the 2nd grade, good at the 3rd grade, and minimal at the 4th grade. In addition, the greatest improvements at the 2nd-grade level were among students who had scored the lowest on the tests administered in the fall.

By the end of the year, the majority of students had improved in their view of reading (Wilsman 1987). These improvements reflected incorporating new ideas about using strategies and reading for meaning, while maintaining the previous viewpoint of reading as an automatic, decoding process. Very few students' improvements reflected an integrated view of reading; that is, recognizing when reading should shift from an automatic to a strategic process.

Results also indicated the value of inservice training and the effectiveness of using the "Storylords" series over a long period of time, accompanied by many teacher-directed lessons.

Use of "Storylords" represents a fundamental change in the way most teachers teach reading. Such a change cannot occur easily or quickly. Educators who wish to switch their way of teaching reading must, among other considerations, allow for enough time to do so.

References

Duffy, C., L.R. Roehler, and U. Mason. (1984). "The Reality and Potential of Comprehension Instruction." In *Comprehension Instruction: Perspectives and Suggestion*, edited by G. Duffy, L.R. Roehler, and U. Mason, Jr. New York: Longman.

Gadow, K.D., and J. Spratkin. (1989). "Field Experiments of Television Violence with Children—For an Environmental Hazard." *Pediatrics* 83, 3: 399-405.

Huesmann, L.R. and N.M. Malamuth, eds. (1986). "Media Violence and Antisocial Behavior." *Journal of Social Issues* 42, 3.

Singer, D.G. (1989). "Children, Adolescents and Television 1989...Televisions Violence—A Critique." *Pediatrics* 83, 3: 445-446.

Wilsman, M.J. (November 1984). "Report of Formative Evaluation for the
Primary Grades Reading Comprehension Project: Children's Video Les-
sons—'Storylords.'" Madison, Wisc.: Wisconsin Educational
Communications Board.

Wilsman, M.J. (June 1987). "'Storylords'", Summative Evaluation Report."
Madison, Wisc.: Wisconsin Public Radio and Television Networks.

*"Storylords" is available for rental or purchase from the Agency for Instruc-
tional Technology in Bloomington, Indiana.

14

Integrating Technologies to Enhance Learning in Science and Mathematics

Regan McCarthy

*O*ther chapters in this book amply describe the use, power, and influence of television, computers, videodiscs, and telecommunications on what and how we learn. But what do we know of the potential of any or all of these technologies when used in combination? Is the effect neutral, cumulative, synergistic?

These questions are neither trivial nor academic. Perhaps nowhere are the effects of technology felt in schools as strongly as in situations where integration of components and media is the rule rather than the exception. The near future of technology appears to be moving rapidly—and somewhat paradoxically—towards both unification and diversification. The increased digital encoding of all forms of data means that all technologies will operate on the same type of input, whereas forms of output can be highly flexible and varied. A single digitized bank of data could be displayable as a television show, a three-dimensional hologram, a computer-generated text on screen or paper, a sound track, or any of a variety of output forms. These hypermedia formats are already being introduced in experimental programs. Our present concern about integrating technology focuses on the best ways to bring diverse sources and forms of information together conveniently and effectively. Ultimately, however, we must deal with a more fundamental question: What information is best conveyed and reinforced by which media, and how do we combine media to enhance learning most effectively?

One attempt to answer these questions began in 1981, when Bank Street College received support from the U.S. Department of Education to develop *The Voyage of the Mimi*, a multimedia program in science and mathematics education now used in thousands of classrooms around the nation. Subsequently, additional information relevant to these questions was obtained from the Mathematics, Science and Technology Teacher Education (MASTTE) Project, a demonstration and research project funded by the National Science Foundation. The MASTTE Project provided training and support and conducted research in 26 school systems nationwide on the content preparation in math and science of elementary teachers, pedagogy and philosophy of science and math teaching, curriculum planning, and management of technology in math and science education. MASTTE used *The Voyage of the Mimi* as a vehicle for its training and support work. Together, these two projects provided us with valuable information about the uses and effects of integrated technologies in science and math learning.

Our early efforts convinced us that integrating media and technology brings considerably more power to learning environments. Children's and teachers' experiences seem to be more expansive, more motivating, more dynamic, and more "real" when integrating technologies than when using technologies independently or not at all.

Integrated Technologies in the *Mimi*

The *Voyage of the Mimi* is a television show in two segments: 13 quarter-hours of adventure story (called episodes) about two researchers and their teenage assistants who are conducting a study of humpback whales aboard a ketch called **Mimi** in the Gulf of Maine; and 13 quarter-hours of documentaries (called expeditions), which explore and expand upon concepts or phenomena depicted in the drama. Accompanying the television segments are *The Overview Guide*, *The Voyage of the Mimi: The Book*, and *Student's* and *Teacher's Guides* for each of four learning modules: *Maps and Navigation*, *Whales and Their Environment*, *Ecosystems*, and *Introduction to Computing*. Each module contains print materials and software for teacher and student use.

The Voyage of the Mimi materials reflect current thinking at Bank Street about how children learn to do scientific investigations, how to bring other resources (such as computers) to bear on this work, and how new and varied media can improve learning. Each type of media is designed to serve a different purpose; as a whole system, the materials present a cohesive and powerful combination of instructional tools.

Television

The television series was designed to be the "prime motivator" of the **Mimi** materials. The theme — whales — was selected because it offers a rich vehicle for science and mathematics, because of its wide appeal to both boys and girls (and adults) in a range of grades, and because it is timely; in short, because it offers a broad base upon which to build the TV shows and related software. Further, the plot was designed to illustrate certain skills and attitudes that are a real part of "doing science." Neither the shows nor the materials discuss formal scientific processes (the scientific method); rather, they convey a disciplined curiosity about scientific and mathematical phenomena. Our belief is that most working scientists were first fascinated with a phenomenon itself (e.g., the highly publicized fascination of Stephen Gould for a snail or Lewis M. Thomas for a cell). Only later were they attracted to the tools and methods for examining the objects that caught their interest.

Software

We designed software programs based on certain assumptions about the uses of technology in learning science and mathematics. First, while the shows are designed to be highly motivating, the computer is the central classroom "attention getter," allowing students to grasp and maintain interest in a topic or theme that the shows present. Second, all software programs contain mathematical and scientific content, although the balance of mathematics and science varies according to the purpose of the software.

Each software program emphasizes a different scientific discipline (e.g., biology), a different mathematical concept (e.g., variables), or both. The disciplines and concepts were selected from the obviously large number of scientific and mathematical areas for several reasons. They are appropriate for elementary students; they offer variety in content; they are adaptable to a range of software formats; and they allow us to show that mathematics and science are partners in the work of understanding natural phenomena. Further, the combinations of specific mathematics concepts and scientific disciplines allow us to reinforce four general skills of scientific investigation: forming and testing hypotheses, predicting, sampling, and generalizing.

Third, **Mimi** software is designed to model software formats commonly used by adult scientists. Consequently, our four learning modules include simulations (*Rescue Mission* in *Maps and Navigation*), modeling software (*Island Survivors* in *Ecosystems*), lab instrumentation (*The Bank Street Lab* in *Whales and Their Environment*), and programming tools (*Whale Search* and other turtle graphic games in *Introduction to Computing*).

Print

Print materials have an equally important and distinctive place in the **Mimi** program. They provide factual information for both teachers and students as well as suggested activities and studies. They also contain probing questions that require time and effort to answer, thus allowing for both continuous reference and slower assimilation of information than either the televised shows or the software. Finally, the print materials provide resources and references for further investigation or study.

Technologies in Combination

According to Sam Gibbon (in press), executive director of the project through which the **Mimi** materials were developed, the combination of media/technologies found in the **Mimi** program has special power to put math and science concepts and problems in "real world" contexts that are highly motivating to students. A dramatic television segment can set the problems, depict engaging characters struggling to solve them (perhaps under considerable dramatic pressure), and then play out the solution as the dramatic conflict is resolved. Documentary episodes and print materials can also provide additional information about the problems under investigation while raising questions that help formulate solutions. Microcomputer software can then present analogous problems for the students to solve.

For example, in Episode 3, the captain of the **Mimi** sets sail toward a dangerous shoal. An electrical problem causes the knotmeter (a nautical speedometer) to malfunction. The captain measures the **Mimi's** speed by timing the boat's passage past a piece of bread thrown in the water. The calculation confirms the captain's suspicions: The boat has been traveling faster than the indicated speed and has therefore gone farther toward the shoals than the captain intended. He must quickly determine the boat's actual position. He triangulates **Mimi's** location by taking compass bearings with the boat's radio direction-finder: Where the bearings cross, there lies the **Mimi**, perilously close to the rocks. Students who watch this episode are absorbed by the dramatic action. Because the mathematics of navigation is central to the resolution of the problem, they remember most of the details. And they are motivated to address the next task: to use *Rescue Mission*, which contains computer-simulated instruments for solving analogous navigation problems. Although the math concepts are difficult, the dramatic demonstration of their value in a life-threatening situation sustains the students' interest through the hard work.

Later in the drama, the **Mimi** is caught in a storm. During the frantic efforts to take down the sails and find a safe harbor, the captain is knocked overboard. He is rescued, but the crew must immediately return to securing the ketch. The captain continues to work to near exhaustion. He has remained in his wet, cold clothing for too long and experiences hypothermia. A speedy attempt to raise his body temperature using standard survival techniques begins. This episode is followed by *Goosebumps*, a documentary on the regulation of body temperature. Students see one of the **Mimi** crew (in his real life persona) at the U.S. Army Arctic Wind Chamber, exposed to various conditions that affect body temperature. Watching the narrator (the 12-year-old protagonist) shiver to keep his core temperature stable as his extremities lose heat elicits sympathy and amazement from student viewers. They become curious about their own body temperatures, wondering if everyone's is the same. By using the temperature probe on the micro-based Bank Street Lab, students easily obtain the answer to this question and several others simultaneously. Measuring the temperature of each student's hand using the temperature sensor of the Bank Street Lab, they quickly explore both the phenomenon of hand temperature, and the characteristics and functions of the Lab. They discover the power of this tool to calibrate, measure, compare, analyze, display, and store their data — in other words, they learn to use technologies in scientific investigations as scientists do.

Integrated Concepts in the Mimi

As noted earlier, all software formats in the **Mimi** materials are designed to engage students in scientific inquiry, just as adult scientists are engaged. But the power of these materials is found not only in the way students are introduced to "real" electronic tools for scientific investigation, but also in the way all parts of these materials are related and held together. The **Mimi** materials are integrated in two ways: first, in the mixture and appropriate use of each medium as it is used to present ideas, images, facts, processes, and tools of scientific and mathematical inquiry; and second, in the conceptual connectedness of the subject matter presented through all media used.

This connectedness is accomplished through the use of themes — whales as the overarching theme, and broad scientific or mathematical concepts (e.g., ecosystems) as themes of modules. The main theme of the television series and the subthemes of the modules, and thus of the print materials and software, are also related. For teachers, this thematic approach makes instruction considerably easier to organize; for students it makes learning seem more natural. With activities driven by questions about broad themes, the irregular and cognitively difficult process of moving from one discipline to the next (e.g., from reading to mathematics to social studies) is minimized.

In working with teachers and staff developers, the MASTTE Project focused on the development of interdisciplinary curriculums in science and mathematics, as well as on linking science and math to other disciplines. MASTTE, too, relied on the use of themes drawn from the **Mimi** materials or from children's interests and experiences. We found a wealth of thematic material in the **Mimi** that could be used as a basis for developing interdisciplinary curriculums. *Energy, Survival, Communications, Whales, Weather,* and *Oceans of Air and Water* are only a few of the broad themes that can be extrapolated from the **Mimi** program and for which the **Mimi** can serve as a springboard for a wide-ranging array of investigations in many disciplines.

The effects of conceptual connectedness — or concept integration — cannot be overstated. For teachers and students alike, the materials "made sense," that is, they were organized in ways consistent with their real, day-to-day experience with phenomena and objects. As Frank Press reminded us, "a walk in the woods is not 45 minutes of rocks, then 45 minutes of trees." It is, especially for children, a whole experience. Conceptual integration such as that found in the **Mimi** program makes it possible for children's investigations to be placed in the context of real, whole experiences.

Research Findings

Many of the aspects of the **Mimi** program are theoretical and philosophical considerations about learning that have been translated into design features of the materials. But how do the materials fare in the classroom?

Two studies have been done on the effects of the **Mimi** program on science and math teaching and learning. The first major research effort began in 1981 by Bank Street's Center for Children and Technology (Char et al. 1983) and concerned formative evaluation of the materials themselves. The second effort began in 1984 with the establishment of the MASTTE Research Component, which reviewed MASTTE participants' uses of the **Mimi** materials and assessed teacher support needs, particularly concerning the use of computers in science and math instruction (Martin 1988; McCarthy 1988).

Char's work tried to answer four basic questions:

- What were the teachers' backgrounds and classroom routines prior to the field test?
- How were materials used and how easily?
- How appealing were the materials to teachers and students?
- How comprehensible were the materials to teachers and students?

Further, Char addressed each of these questions from multiple perspectives: according to the perceptions of teachers, students, and Bank Street's own staff of researchers. For example, to obtain a collective picture of student comprehension of a piece of software, teachers were asked what aspects seemed unclear to students; students were asked what questions they had about the materials; and students took a comprehension test that focused on specific software tasks that seem to be generally problematic for children. Data from seven measures were obtained that covered teacher background, in-class usage, and materials evaluations, and involved questionnaires, student and teacher interviews, and classroom observation.

With regard to teacher background and preparation, we found three characteristics that influenced how much the materials were used. First, we consistently found that the materials were used more often, and student users were more satisfied with the materials, when a microcomputer was regularly available in the classroom. Second, we found that the role teachers assumed significantly affected use. Teachers who used software only to demonstrate to students were, as might be expected, associated with a significant drop in student interaction. Finally, we found that teachers' prior experience with a microcomputer did not greatly affect software use, although the degree to which teachers themselves understood the mathematics and science concepts in the materials was highly influential.

With respect to appeal and comprehension of the materials, we found that the television shows had high appeal, held the interest of children (and most teachers), and transmitted useful and accurate information about science, mathematics, and scientists at work. Research showed that the software required the greatest change in teaching strategies and that three factors affected its comprehensibility and appeal to teachers and students: (1) teachers' understanding of the software itself (what it does, how it works, what concepts seem to be problematic for children); (2) the structure of the software (less structured software such as the Lab poses more difficulties regarding classroom management than more structured software such as Rescue Mission); and (3) the level of student understanding of the concepts inherent in the software, as well as the tasks required to use it effectively.

Formative research indicated two other factors that affect the use of **Mimi** materials, but over which we could have little influence: (1) the science background — whether formally or informally acquired — of teachers and (2) the individual teacher's preferred teaching style. Teachers with strong backgrounds in science and mathematics were clearly able to use these materials more effectively. With regard to teaching style, we found that child-centered teachers were more effective in using this technology than were teacher-centered teachers. Both these findings speak to the pre-service training of teachers, as well as to the general interests and preferences of individual teachers using **Mimi** materials.

MASTTE research generally corroborated the findings of the **Mimi** formative research. In addition, we obtained several interesting findings about the use of materials, changes in teacher and student attitudes toward science and mathematics, and the effects of using the **Mimi** program on the classroom environment.

MASSTE research on the use of the materials found that teachers used integrated technologies in many different ways. Some used the video portion first, others the software, and still others the print materials. Some showed the videos slowly over time with computer-based or laboratory experiences interspersed. Still others used the materials in disciplines other than science first, for example, as a language arts experience or for social studies. These variations reflect both the versatility of the materials and the inclination of teachers to work initially in their most familiar disciplines. Ultimately, all teachers used all media and all increased instruction in mathematics and science. However, the integration of both media and content throughout the materials afforded teachers and students greater options.

We also found that this flexibility helped teachers to grapple with their own limitations in science and mathematics. Many of the teachers we worked with were as naive as their students about science and mathematics. (This phenomenon is not peculiar to MASTTE teachers, having been reported by David Hawkins [1972] and others who are concerned with barriers to adult learning.) After extensive training and support, MASTTE teachers reported excitement and surprise at their increasing interest in these subject areas; a substantial number began science studies, although we believe this is more attributable to MASTTE training than to the **Mimi** program. Especially significant was the ease with which some of the project's more technology-phobic teachers began to use all the technology/media in the materials.

Students showed similar enthusiasm, largely because the materials are inherently motivating, but also because the materials encourage pedagogical changes that allow children to do what adults do: be flexible in using resources, tools, and activities to solve problems. Students worked in all kinds of arrangements: alone, in small groups, in large groups; with teacher assistance, with peer assistance, and with expert help; with computers, with laboratory materials, and with common, everyday objects.

Overwhelmingly, the feeling in the classrooms we observed was that when the **Mimi** program was used, it pervaded the life of the classroom. In this sense, all parts of the classroom were integrated into the scientific and mathematical investigations underway. This led to some interesting changes in classroom atmosphere. While watching the video portions, children invariably became more relaxed. Seating arrangements became informal, occasional comments among students about events in the episode were heard, and a perceptible shift in teacher and student exchanges was seen. Since "video first" was the predominant mode of entering **Mimi** activities, this casual and comfortable atmosphere frequently led to more student-initiated activity and especially enhanced small-group work in classrooms.

We also found some constraints to the uses of integrated technologies that are probably typical across the nation. These are: (1) declining budgets, with a resulting low priority given to innovation in school budgets; (2) lack of personnel qualified to train teachers to use integrated technologies appropriately; (3) resistance among teachers to new technology; (4) the rudimentary state of communications software; and (5) the nascent state of research on the effects of technology on learning. Perhaps the greatest obstacle, however, is none of these. It may be that schools lack models for evaluating their use of these technologies. The availability of some of the most accessible and useful technologies (including telecommunications) for teachers is so recent that we have only begun to accumulate the research findings and practitioner wisdom to inform us about when, how, or even why various technologies are appropriate in mathematics and science education.

We also found powerful obstacles to interdisciplinary instruction. Teachers rarely had the flexibility to institutionalize MASTTE/**Mimi** program approaches to science and math instruction. A range of forces — state syllabi, departmentalization, standardized testing, and other rigidly discipline-based practices and structures made it difficult for teachers to apply this innovation more broadly despite substantial evidence that interdisciplinary instruction is of benefit to students and teachers. From measures of teacher and student satisfaction, student performance (grades, peer and expert review), and frequency and duration of science and math instruction, the picture is clear: interdisciplinary instruction — integrated conceptually and technologically — is highly motivating and engaging, and leads to more sustained participation in science and math.

The MASTTE/**Mimi** program experiment has shown us the promise and potential of moving toward integrating technologies in the classroom. Despite the uncertainties of using innovative technologies, we have seen unquestionable benefits to students and teachers, even in these early applications. But underlying the issue of integrated technologies is another, more fundamental question about which we have only indirect knowledge: Is the medium really the message? In other words, is the value of integrated technologies essentially in the variety and flexibility they introduce into instruction, regardless of the content of that instruction, or is it related intimately to the information we are trying to convey? In the case of *The Voyage of the **Mimi***, it would be difficult to separate the functional benefits of the hardware from the substance embedded in the television shows, software, and print materials. As mentioned before, the relation between the content and processes was carefully considered by the developers so that the particular medium used to convey content is direct and clear. This design factor may be the reason the **Mimi** program is such a strong example of effective integration.

References

Char, E., J. Hawkins, K. Sheingold, and T. Roberts, (February 1983). *The Voyage of the **Mimi**: Classroom Case Studies of Software, Video, and Print Materials*. New York: Bank Street College.

Gibbon, S., Jr. (in press). "Learning and Instruction in the Information Age." In *What Curriculum for the Information Age?*, edited by M.A. White. Hillsdale, NJ: Erlbaum.

Greenfield, P.M. (1984). *Mind and Media*. Cambridge, Mass.: Harvard University Press.

Hawkins, D. (1972). *A Report of Research on Critical Barriers to the Learning and Understanding of Elementary Science*. Prepared for the National Science Foundation. Boulder, Colo.: University of Colorado.

Martin, L. (1988). *The Mathematics, Science and Technology Teacher Education Project: Research Summary*. Prepared for the National Science Foundation. N.Y.: Bank Street College of Education.

McCarthy, R. (1988). *The Mathematics, Science and Technology Teacher Education Project Executive Summary*. Prepared for the National Science Foundation. N.Y.: Bank Street College of Education.

15

Learning Dramas: An Alternative Curricular Approach to Using Computers with At-Risk Students

Stanley Pogrow

*A*re you beginning to have second thoughts about your investment in computers—particularly if you purchased them in the hope that they would significantly enhance the learning of at-risk students? Now that the initial euphoria is over for you and the students, are you seeing a substantial change in the quality of their work? Have they become sophisticated learners? Now that they have word processed have they become good writers? Is the stuff starting to look like expensive worksheets? Has the expenditure significantly lessened the at-risk problem in your school/district?

While some are having success with using computers, many concerns are well founded. Research is finding that conventional computer use has little overall effect with at-risk students beyond the 3rd grade, and may even widen learning gaps.[1] Indeed, the at-risk problem has substantially increased over the past decade while educators have spent hundreds of millions of dollars on computers. Seven years ago I started out to develop a more effective approach to using computers with at-risk students—particularly during the critical years in grades 4-7. The result is a new curricular approach that combines two of the oldest pedagogical traditions—Socratic dialogue and drama—with the newest forms of technology and learning theory. The techniques that emerged for using computers with at-risk students are the opposite of conventional approaches to using computers and have been demonstrated on a large scale to be very effective.

The Conventional Curricular Approach to Using Computers

Conventional approaches to using software rely on its explicit goal to produce learning. For example, if one were teaching students the concept of "average," one would use software explicitly designed to provide practice in that instructional goal. Such software would be expected to independently increase the students' knowledge of calculating and using averages. The only curricular concern would be to coordinate the use of that software with the learning objective of the school's content. This is usually referred to as integrating computers into the curriculum.

Using software with the explicit goal of teaching content is most commonly referred to as "computer-assisted instruction" or CAI. While CAI is usually associated with drill and practice, the new computer tools, such as word processors, spreadsheets, and simulations generally end up being used as CAI

---

[1]Research reviews of the effectiveness of CAI such as Bangert-Drowns, Kulik, and Kulik (1985) and Niemiec and Walberg (1987) find that the major effects from CAI have been demonstrated at the early elementary grade levels and then decline rapidly. Haller, Child, and Walberg (1988) found that metacognition (without technology) has twice the effect of CAI. Finally, Hativa (1988) found that when high and low performing students both use CAI, the technology widens learning gaps. Nor is there any evidence that word processing improves the writing of at-risk students.

because the goal of the software is expected to produce learning.[2] Word processors are expected to increase students' writing ability, and a simulation of chemical titration is expected to enhance students' knowledge of the specific chemical reactions that are modeled. Learning is presumed to occur when students successfully use the software.

The belief that successful use of software can produce substantial amounts of learning has so dominated the use of computers since their inception that there are virtually no articles on alternative curricular approaches to using them. If one believes that computers can enhance learning by simply integrating software into the curriculum, there's no need or incentive to rework the curriculum or change instructional approaches, nor is there any reason to develop alternative, more sophisticated, curricular approaches. Unfortunately, integrating literal uses of software into the curriculum has generally failed to help at-risk students except at the earliest grade levels.

There are two problems with relying on the explicit goal of software with at-risk students. First, the approach is simply not practical. Matching software goals to the ever increasing number of curricular objectives, and negotiating with all the different vendors, is a logistical nightmare. The more objectives that students need help with, the worse the logistics. The second problem is that CAI incorrectly assumes that the fundamental learning problem of at-risk students is that they have not internalized concepts because they simply haven't had enough practice using them, or that the practice provided is too boring to have an effect. The explicit goal approach to using software assumes that providing additional computer-based practice increases the chances that the concepts will be internalized.

The root of the learning problems of at-risk students in grades 4-7, however, is probably not lack of practice or boredom. Brown (1982) concludes that the primary cause of learning problems in at-risk students is inadequate metacognition skills. (A simple definition of metacognition is the ability to consciously apply and test strategies when solving problems and engaging in normal thinking activities such as reading comprehension.) My own conclusion is that an additional key problem is that at-risk students do not understand

---

[2]Most computer specialists will object to characterizing tools such as word processors as CAI because they go to great pains to distinguish their use from drill-and-practice applications. At the same time, there is no functional difference between how word processors tend to be used in schools and how drill-and-practice software is used. Both depend on the function of the software to produce learning.

In addition, the term "CAI" will be used even though many make fine distinctions between that and other terms such as "Computer-Based Education," or CBE, and "Tool Use." These and other terms used all share the same basic characteristic of primary reliance on the explicit goal of software.

"understanding." The students have no idea how to think about the types of ideas used in school to the extent that they do not even seem to know what it means to understand something that involves the use of symbols (Pogrow 1990a). Thus, CAI solves the wrong problem. Simply practicing a problem more efficiently on a computer screen is not going to help students with metacognition and understanding deficits. Students who do not read books with comprehension, and who do not spontaneously metacognize about what they are reading with regular text, will not do so with information presented on a computer screen. Curricular approaches that depend on the literal goal of software cannot help these problems. CAI can only help those students who already spontaneously construct linkages and understandings, i.e. those students who are already performing well.

A Learning Drama Approach to Using Software

The result of my work to develop the thinking and understanding skills of at-risk students is a thinking skills program called HOTS (Pogrow 1988a, 1990a.) Extensive experience with at-risk students led to the development of this curricular approach to using computers that combines the use of software, Socratic dialogue, and dramatic techniques in ways suggested by information processing theories of learning. The resulting techniques are called "Learning Dramas." These techniques have been demonstrated to produce larger gains than remedial approaches with Chapter 1 students in grades 4-7. The results were validated by the review panel for the Federal National Diffusion Networks.

Definition of Learning Dramas

The five key characteristics of learning dramas are:
a) Instead of using the software to teach concepts, the learning occurs indirectly from special conversations about learning to use the software. The explicit goal of the software has nothing to do with what is taught or learned.
b) There is virtually no discussion of technical issues about how to use software. Students are expected to figure that out on their own from textual clues. Discussions focus on ideas designed to develop key thinking skills.
c) Dramatic techniques are used in the lessons to heighten the students' curiosity and motivation.

106

d) Teachers are trained in how to systematically probe student answers in a Socratic manner to produce understanding.

e) Thinking is not "taught." Rather, it evolves from extensive, consistent patterns of visual interaction about ideas.

In learning dramas, the explicit goal of the software is viewed only as a student motivator, an interesting goal for them to achieve. Learning comes from Socratic conversations around other aspects of the software. Words and concepts in the menus and instructions on the screen provide opportunities to invent questions that enable students to practice key thinking activities, regardless of whether such questions help students achieve the goal of the software. These are called "invented" or "incidental" questions.

Specific content objectives are built indirectly into these discussions. Situations are created in which it is important to talk about the content concept as a means to an end. Suppose, for example, you wanted students to learn the concept of average. Instead of using software designed to teach averages (a CAI approach), a learning drama approach would find a piece of software that would be of interest to the students, and around which a situation could be invented that would require the use of averages. Any problem that produces a numerical score and requires the use of a strategy can be used. The learning drama scenario would then be as follows:

> Teachers would tell the students: "In the game we played yesterday you got some very good scores, but also some poor ones. That means that you were guessing. If, on the other hand, you have a good strategy you will get good *overall* scores." After students played the game for a few times, teachers would then tell students: "An average tells you how good your *overall* score is and, therefore, how good your strategy is." Teachers would then quickly show students how to calculate an average, and have students go back to playing the game. Thereafter, the teacher would discuss with students whether their averages were improving, and what strategies they were using to get better averages.

Tying the concept of average to an interesting problem-solving activity using software intended to "teach" something else produces greater understanding and retention with just a small amount of discussion than continued CAI practice with software explicitly intended to teach the concept of average. In addition, as students read clues and talk about their strategies, they are practicing reading comprehension and metacognition, which simultaneously develops their reading and thinking skills. Indeed, one of the surprising findings from the research is that this approach is so powerful that you do not need to cover that many objectives in this manner to enhance the learning of all content objectives in the classroom.

The Importance of the Conversations

To produce substantial amounts of learning, the invented conversations cannot just be talk for the sake of talking, or thinking for the sake of thinking. The conversations must consistently model key thinking skills. Information processing theory suggests that the following thinking skills be focused on:

a. **Metacognition** - Consciously applying strategies to solve problems;
b. **Inference from context** - Figuring out unknown words and information from the surrounding information;
c. **Decontextualization** - Generalizing ideas from one context to another;
d. **Information synthesis** - Combining information from a variety of sources and identifying the key pieces of information needed to solve a problem.

While the terminology sounds intimidating, learning dramas turn them into fun for both the students and the teacher. The curriculum develops these thinking skills in the following ways:

Metacognition is taught through asking students what strategy they used for solving a problem, how they know the strategy is a good one, what strategies they found that did not work, how they could tell if a strategy did not work, and what a better strategy might be, etc.

Inference from context is modeled in two ways. The first technique is to have students read a computerized twist-a-plot story that combines text with graphics and allows students to control the direction of the story. These dynamic features increase the students' absorption of what they read on the screen, particularly if it is an adventure story that will interest students and involve them in the suspense of finding the outcome. Teachers then heighten student involvement by introducing the setting in a dramatic fashion—such as warning the students that they will encounter many dangers in the story. The dramatic element builds high levels of engagement—a prerequisite for thinking.

The second technique involves words in key places that students do not understand. (It does not matter which words, or whether the words are in the students' regular curriculum.) Students are told that every time they come to a word they do not understand, they should: a) write down the sentence in which it appears, b) circle the word, and c) call the teacher over and make a guess about what the word means. The teacher lists the sentences the students have pulled out of the story on the board and asks students to explain what they think the circled words mean from the readings and pictures, and why. Students are also asked to compare their predictions about what twists the story will take with what actually happened.

The conversations begin and student answers are probed. These rich conversations model prediction comprehension processes that good readers spontaneously engage in, and provide experience in information synthesis and metacognition, as well as in inference from context.

The second techniques can be used around any piece of software where unknown or ambiguous words appear in the instructions. Teachers constantly ask students to figure out what the unknown words mean and what strategy they used for figuring it out. The visual clues make it easier initially for students to build up confidence in their inference skills. Inference then becomes a normal part of learning how to use any piece of software.

Decontextualization is also taught in two ways. The first uses words that students are familiar with from their everyday experience and has them make predictions about what they are likely to do in the context of a particular program. For example, the graphics program *DAZZLE DRAW* has a menu choice called "Flood Fill." Students are asked to predict what will happen if they make that choice based on what they know about the word "flood." Students then go to the computers to test their predictions ("Flood Fill" fills an area of the screen with a chosen color.)

The second technique involves discussing concepts with several different meanings in several different pieces of software. For example, perspective is discussed when flying a hot-air balloon, writing a story, and viewing a given situation. Students are asked about how the uses of the concept in the different programs are the same and different.

Information synthesis is done by creating situations where students have to use information from a variety of sources, or several different types of information, to solve a problem or develop a strategy. For example, in the program *Where in the World is Carmen San Diego* by Broderbund, students have to combine information from an almanac, a dictionary, and the screen to solve a case.

Developing Curricular Materials

Curriculum is developed by taking a piece of software that will be of interest to students (games and adventure stories are always good), and inventing a series of questions that will provide practice in all of the above and link concepts to other pieces of software. In a very popular simulation called *Oregon Trail*, the explicit goal is for students to reach Oregon along the Old Oregon Trail, which pioneers used to travel from Independence, Missouri to Oregon City, Oregon. They have to budget food and supplies appropriately in order to make it safely through a variety of problems that the computer throws at them, including attacks, bad weather, and floods.

The learning drama questions discussed by students are incidental to the goal of reaching Oregon. They are based on words or phrases in the instructions. The questions are asked to initiate discussions that provide practice in the four key thinking skills. The quality of discussions about the answers to these questions is far more important to the learning process than the quality or successful use of the software. Indeed, the newer, technologically jazzy version of *Oregon Trail* is not as good for learning dramas as the old, black-and-white, classic version.[3] It is this focus on discussions around tangential questions, which model key thinking processes, that distinguishes learning dramas from conventional CAI.

While using technology expressly to create a setting around which to invent other types of learning seems counter-intuitive, the success of this approach has been demonstrated by Dr. John Bransford (1989) at Vanderbilt. Bransford used laserdisk technology to show a segment of Indiana Jones jumping across a pit (i.e., to set an interesting visual context that was familiar to students), followed by a discussion of the physical forces and mathematics that makes such an act possible. He found that using the visual setting provided by the technology to set the context for a follow-up discussion was a more effective way to teach math to at-risk students than using only technology or one-on-one instruction.

Applying Dramatic Techniques

Learning dramas must, of course, be dramatic. The dramatic element is designed to engage and intrigue students. Teachers often wear costumes, tell jokes, etc. In addition, much as a good stage drama involves the audience in the situation and emotion of the story and characters, learning dramas are created

---

[3]The new version of *Oregon Trail* is far more elaborate than the older version. It uses color graphics and provides many more decision-making situations. Unfortunately, its potential for metacognition is much less since it takes an hour for students to find out if they have successfully reached Oregon as compared to ten minutes in the old version. Since metacognition requires students to speculate about whether a strategy did or did not work in terms of getting to Oregon, the new version is of little value. This illustrates how advances in software can in fact be detrimental to the development of key thinking activities once those key activities have been identified.

110

to get students emotional about the tasks they are involved in. Such emotion deepens the learning process. Every piece of software has unintended uses that a clever curriculum develops into dramatic situations. For example, there is a popular program called "Word Master," in which students have to turn a pointer to match words on the screen. You have to match words quickly or you lose. There is a word on the bottom that indicates the matching rule (i.e., synonyms, antonyms). The intended CAI use of the software is a vocabulary drill-and-practice program. In the HOTS curriculum, this software is used to teach the importance of understanding rules and using clues to determine what the rules are. The sequence of lessons works as follows:

> On the first day, the teacher sets the program to match antonyms and points out the word antonym on the bottom of the screen. The students proceed to play the game and get good scores. The next day, the students come in confident that they are going to get very high scores. The teacher, however, has switched the computers to want synonym matches and does not tell the students. The students go to their computers and quickly become dismayed and start to complain that the machines are broken. Their natural certainty about how to master the environment quickly turns to feelings of outrage that the computers are not working. The teacher calmly explains that the computer is working perfectly, and if they think carefully, the information they need is available. When finally convinced that things are not going to work, they start to look at the screen carefully and notice that the word on the bottom is now "synonym." Students then make the adjustment, get good scores, and feel proud of themselves. The next day, the teacher engages them in a conversation about the importance of words in understanding what the rules are and how developing strategies depends on first reading the available information carefully, or in the case of the classroom, listening to the information provided by the teacher. This is learning in the context of very high drama, with excitement turning to despair, then once again to excitement and joy.

After that day, the students are unlikely to forget about the importance of rules and are attentive during future discussions about rules. Letting students experience, and discover on their own, the importance of concepts in dramatic situations is more effective than lecturing.

Research has demonstrated that interaction about ideas in socially meaningful situations is critical to their internalization (Vygotsky 1978).

Choreographing situations that generate passion about new ways to think about ideas leads to powerful forms of learning.

Of course, developing a curriculum in which students discover the need for a concept and become involved in figuring out how to manipulate it is far more difficult than simply telling them what to do. In learning dramas, the situations must be carefully choreographed.

Implementing Socratic Dialogue Techniques

At the heart of learning dramas are the conversations between teacher and student and among students. Even the best curriculum only provides the potential for appropriate forms of conversation to exist. While the curriculum provides the questions to initiate the conversations, the teacher's follow-up questions and reactions are even more critical. Teachers must react to student questions and answers in ways that maintain the types of ambiguities, probes, and clues that lead students to construct meaning on their own. If teachers do not question or respond to student answers appropriately, the most sophisticated curriculum and software become rote learning activities.

The most misunderstood concept about the use of technology with at-risk students is that producing sophisticated learning is a function of the sophistication of conversation that surrounds the use of the technology—not the sophistication of the technology. That was true of television, it is true of calculators and lab experiments (McPartland and Wu 1988), it is true of computers, and will be true of the next generation of shiny boxes—no matter how powerful or how many flashing lights they have.

A major emphasis of learning dramas is training teachers in Socratic dialogue techniques. Teachers have to learn how to be a guide rather than a provider of information, to listen to student answers in terms of understanding (rather than right or wrong answers), and to probe student responses to help the students construct their own understanding.

Becoming skilled in engaging students in Socratic dialogue is not easy, even with good curriculum and a good system. Unfortunately, I cannot begin to describe in words why it is so difficult to listen for understanding and then to spark understanding with follow-up questions. This is the most critical of all skills—and the least practiced in American education. It takes a week of practice to train even good teachers to start to become Socratic. The training techniques used are modelled after how actors and actresses learn to interpret their roles. Just as performers learn how to interact through practice readings, teachers spend a week teaching lessons from the HOTS curriculum to each other. Over the course of a week, each teacher encounters each of the key dialogue situations many times. At the end of each teaching there is a debriefing as to whether the appropriate Socratic strategy was used in each situation. Tying the learning of the techniques to specific experiences is as important for teachers as it is for students.

The practice and feedback gained during training enable teachers to become metacognitive about their teaching; that is, they learn how to examine what they are doing and consciously reflect on the appropriateness of how they handle a given situation. The hardest situation to learn to deal with is when students give logically correct, but unexpected and inconvenient, answers. Although good teachers can effectively implement the techniques immediately, they report that it takes a year of monitoring themselves before the techniques become automatic. At the same time, student involvement in learning dramas produces widespread learning gains so that it is only necessary to train a core group of teachers in the Socratic techniques, a core that will at some point reach most students.

Why Are Learning Dramas So Effective?

I have suggested that you should spend extra money to buy computers, you should spend more money and buy software, and then you should use them in ways that they were not intended to be used. Why go to all this expense when you will still have to go to the trouble of developing curriculum and training teachers in complicated pedagogical techniques? The justification for this is that the combination of curricular techniques and Socratic dialogue around technology has been demonstrated to be more effective with at-risk students than literal uses of software, or non-technology-based interventions.[4]

The question remains, however, as to why it works so well. Indeed, I was initially surprised that a set of techniques designed to develop thinking skills was producing gains on standardized test scores that doubled the national average for Chapter 1 students. How could such techniques produce substantial gains in content learning without extensive linkage to the curriculum or test?

After seven years of working with the techniques (there are now close to 20,000 students in the HOTS program), and talking to teachers and students,

---

[4]In the report to the National Diffusion Network, the results showed that HOTS students gained almost twice as much in reading and math as the national average for Chapter 1 students. Since that study was conducted, a newer version of the techniques has been developed, and sites are reporting gains that exceed those produced in the original study. In addition, when one teacher compared the use of the HOTS techniques against a commercial CAI drill-and-practice program in two of her groups, HOTS students did better in reading and math on the vendor's own test.

the following conclusions have been reached that have general implications for curriculum development:

1. Learning dramas stimulate complex thinking processes much in the same manner as children learn to talk—by imitating adult actions. Social imitation is one of the most powerful forms of learning. Students will imitate the behaviors and actions of adults if they are consistently modeled in situations that the students deem significant. By constantly modeling the processes that are critical to knowledge transfer and fundamental to content learning, learning dramas stimulate imitative behaviors. Indeed, some teachers report that students even imitate their hand gestures.

Teaching thinking strategies will not work because they will be viewed in isolation as all the other content is. Rather, the act of thinking in a certain way must be experienced sufficiently in social situations of interest to the student that it becomes acculturated.

2. There does not appear to be a need to build extensive content objectives into the learning drama curriculum or to use integration or scope-and-sequence techniques. Providing extensive experience in applying some objectives in more sophisticated ways enables students to learn the other content objectives of the classroom far more effectively the first time they are taught. Once students understand what it means to link ideas, they seem to spontaneously construct the types of understandings that enable them to learn all content better.

3. Learning dramas simultaneously generate multiple types of learning.

4. Learning dramas need to be maintained over time in order for students to internalize the key thinking skills. The best approach with at-risk students in grades 4-7 seems to be to provide learning dramas in self-contained settings, 35 minutes a day for 2 years. Thereafter, students are able to benefit from learning dramas built into content learning, and will benefit more from traditional curricular and CAI techniques. In other words, learning dramas enable students to eventually benefit from other good curricular approaches.

The learning drama curricular approach is very flexible but requires high levels of discipline and creativity. It can be adapted to meet many needs and incorporate new techniques. The HOTS curriculum designed for Chapter 1 students is also effective with gifted students—albeit at earlier grade levels.

Learning dramas can also be used to construct content courses and thereby develop thinking-in-content skills. The HOTS project is currently developing a two-year thinking-in-mathematics course for the middle school. The goal is to extend the learning drama approach to the learning of traditional mathematics objectives. The course will use a completely different

114

approach to mathematics, and will seek to increase content learning through problem solving. All activities will involve the four key thinking skills. In addition, all the activities will be organized around 4-10 key mathematical themes, such as proportional reasoning.

The HOTS project is also developing new software that enables students to create their own math problems if they are able to organize the language needed to express them. This will allow mathematical understanding to be derived from language comprehension.

The first year of the planned curriculum should be available for the GS by 7/91, and for IBM and Macintosh by 7/92. Schools can also extend learning dramas to other grade levels or content areas on their own. Specific curriculums and interaction procedures must be developed and learned. Developing original learning dramas requires: a) a team of individuals to select the key thinking activities that are to be modeled, b) selecting software to be used, and c) writing the key questions that are to be used on a daily basis over a 1-2 year period to model the key thinking activities. A detailed guide is available to help districts with this process (Pogrow 1990b).

Why not Use Books Instead of Computers?

If the heart of learning dramas is Socratic dialogue that models key thinking processes, why use expensive technology?

Good teachers have used Socratic techniques with books for several thousand years. While books will continue to be the fundamental learning tool, computers offer several potential advantages as a setting for Socratic conversations—particularly for at-risk students without extensive problem-solving experience. In addition to the motivational effects, computers provide: a) a way of mixing different learning modalities together and providing students with the flexibility to draw upon whichever modality, be it graphic, tactile, or aural, they initially feel comfortable with, b) a dynamic way for students to test ideas at the speed at which they can think of them, with immediate feedback, c) feedback with interpretation critical to understanding the correctness of answers and strategies, and d) a private environment where students uncertain of their abilities can first test their ideas before having to discuss them publicly. These advantages, however, are only a potential. They require state-of-the-art curriculums and conversation techniques. The ultimate goal of learning dramas is to develop a student who loves to read and discuss books.

Criticisms of the Learning Drama Approach

The biggest critics of these techniques are technology advocates. Many leaders of the technology movement have reacted to the findings of effectiveness by accusing HOTS of not being a technology program since it emphasizes other instructional and curricular techniques. The work is also criticized because of uncertainty about what proportion of the gain is being caused by the computer. Rather than celebrating the fact that students are learning, the technology advocates worry that if educators find out that the technology does not produce learning by itself, and/or that the sophistication of conversation is the key, educators will not use technology. Researchers keep trying to show that computers can produce learning by themselves. Unfortunately, this leads to simplistic patterns of use that cannot possibly enhance learning in most students (Pogrow 1988b).

Response to Criticisms

I do not know to what extent the technology is responsible for the learning gains reported in the HOTS program. What I do know is that the combination of techniques produces high levels of learning in at-risk students. Producing learning in at-risk students requires far more sophisticated understanding of the nature and cause of the learning problem—regardless of whether or not computers are used. The problem is so complex that no simple conception, or direct use of technology, will solve it. Learning dramas is but one approach. The bottom line is that if we can develop techniques that work, educators will adopt them even if we cannot prove that the technology is doing it.

Summary

The obvious way to use technology with at-risk students is not the best way! This means that there is an opportunity and need to develop new and more creative forms of curriculum. Producing sophisticated learning requires sophisticated interventions. We have to stop viewing technology as machines, and teacher training as learning how to use them. These are powerful potentials that require more, not less, sophisticated curriculum and pedagogy. Curriculum specialists must stop deferring to technologists, and technologists must stop viewing themselves as specialists while paying only lip service to the process of pedagogy and learning outcomes. We must all, in short, combine our points of view if we are to best apply the power of technology, new theories of cognition, and learning traditions from other disciplines, cultures, and art forms. And we must recognize that a roundabout but sophisticated approach to using technology may improve the learning of at-risk students much more than direct routes.

Coming Attractions from the HOTS Project

Self Training Videotapes

Videotapes will be available by 10/90 to provide training in the curriculum development and teacher training techniques used in HOTS. The teaching videotapes are intended for either classroom teachers or computer teachers who will be using the curriculum on an occasional basis with their students. Those using HOTS to produce gains in gifted, Chapter 1, or learning disabled students should still go through a regular training session and not rely on the videotapes.

Middle School Mathematics Course

An extension of HOTS techniques to a two-year mathematics course for middle school students, this course will combine computers and Socratic dialogue to teach middle school math objectives. In addition, a new type of math software will be developed for the course. The course will take a unique approach to teaching mathematics. Projected availability date, 9/91.

References

Bangert-Drowns, R., J. Kulik, and C. Kulik. (Summer 1985). "Effectiveness of Computer-Based Education In Secondary Schools." *Journal of Computer-Based Instruction.*

Bransford, J. et al. (1989). "Mathematical Thinking." To be published in *Teaching for Evaluating Mathematical Problem-Solving,* edited by R. Charles and E. Silver. Reston, Va.: National Council of Teachers of Mathematics.

Brown, A. (April 1982). "Inducing Strategic Learning from Text by Means of Informed, Self-Control Training." *Topics in Learning and Learning Disabilities.*

Haller, E., D. Child, and H. Walberg. (December 1988). "Can Comprehension be Taught? A Quantitative Synthesis of 'Metacognitive' Studies." *Educational Researcher.*

Hativa, N. (Fall 1988). "Computer-Based Drill and Practice in Arithmetic: Widening the Gap Between High- and Low-Achieving Students." - *American Educational Research Journal.*

McPartland, J., and S. Wu. (July 1988). "Instructional Practice in the Middle Grades: National Variations and Effects." Baltimore, Md.: Johns Hopkins University .

Niemiec, R., and H. Walberg. (1987). "The Comparative Effects of Computer-Assisted Instruction: A Synthesis of Reviews." *Journal of Educational Computing Research.*

Pogrow, S. (April 1988a). " A Thinking Skills Approach to Enhance the Performance of Elementary At-Risk Students: Experience from the HOTS Program." *Educational Leadership* 45, 7.

Pogrow, S. (January 1990a). "Challenging At-Risk Students: Results from the HOTS Program." *Phi Delta Kappan.*

Pogrow, S. (in press, October 1990b). *A HOTS Guide to Using Computers with At-Risk Students.* Scholastic, Inc.

Pogrow, S. (1988b). "The Computer Coverup." *Electronic Learning.*

Vygotsky, L.S. (1978). *Mind in Society: The Development of Higher Psychological Precesses.* Boston, Mass.: Harvard University Press.

16

Technology In Early Childhood Education

Barbara Bowman

*T*hat we are in the midst of a technological revolution is apparent even to those of us who never go to the moon, or bounce sound off satellites, or design microchips smaller than fingernails. The 20th century has brought a series of technological advances that have revolutionized how we live. The changes and benefits of the new technologies are conspicuous in every aspect of our lives. Televisions, telephones, computers, and the interface among them are rapidly expanding our ability to process large quantities of information, to communicate with one another more directly, to do hard labor more easily, and to challenge ourselves with a greater variety of problems.

The new wave of technology has created a large demand for workers who are able to use the tools being developed and to develop new ones. This demand is expected to swell as the newly created tools themselves become sources of new knowledge. Scientific and technical competence is essential to American competitiveness in worldwide economic and political arenas. And because computers are the cornerstones for technological advancement, schools have the responsibility to prepare children to use them.

At present, schools are failing to produce the scientists and technicians who will carry the United States into the 21st century. American children lag behind children from China, Japan, and many European countries in mathematics test scores. The National Assessment of Educational Progress (NAEP) reported recently that more than half the nation's 17-year-olds are inadequately prepared for jobs that require technical skills, or for matriculation in college-level science courses. The NEAP report suggests that the pedagogy of early childhood programs may be responsible, in part, for this poor performance (ASCD 1988). Stigler (1988) noted that Japanese superiority over American children in mathematics is real, large, broad, and appears early. How can American schools better prepare children to be competitive in the technology race ahead? First, schools must recognize that all children must be knowledge-able on all facets of math and science and their applications. Shamos (1988) pointed out the impossibility of training all children to the highest levels of science achievement, much less to the highest level in all the disciplines that underlie modern technology. He wrote that schools should build for the future by developing an appreciation for science in their students. He agrees with others who contend that students do not study science because it is useful, but rather because it brings them pleasure.

The goal of technology education should be to motivate children to enjoy their studies as well as to be skillful at them, thereby ensuring that they will want to use their skills for amusement and fun as well as to pass tests. To blend competency with interest, basic skills with creativity, and hard work with joy is a challenge not just for colleges and universities, not just for middle schools and high schools, but for early childhood educators as well.

Second, schools must recognize that technology is not an unmitigated blessing and be aware of potential dangers. At best, technology creates tools that can be used in creative ways, augmenting the capabilities of the user. The benefit lies in how the tool is used. The importance of the telephone is not in its capacity to send and receive messages, but in the value of the communication between participants. The importance of computers and word processing programs is in its capacity to encode personal thoughts. There is a real danger that as technological tools become more sophisticated they may usurp human creativity, replacing it with a bland diet of pre-programmed accomplishments. A computer program that structures children's writing so there is little room for their personal meaning is a threat not an asset, even if the product is gram-matically correct. Young children must be encouraged to think of technology as a tool they can guide and direct according to their own interests.

The Current Status of Technology Education in Schools

The first round of applications of computer technology in schools has been incredibly sterile. Most have focused on computer-assisted instruction (CAI), an instructional strategy that uses a computer in place of paper and pencil. Hence the term electronic work sheet has been applied to these applications. Solomon and Gardner (1986) suggested that educators who use computers in this way seem to expect the computer to have a magical enhancement quality that adds "something" extra to traditional methods. According to Solomon and Gardner, however, "When everything else is indeed held constant, save the medium, not much of an effect can be observed."

So what do children learn when we put work sheets on computers? At best they may learn that technology promotes the same old rote learning, but inside a box instead of on a piece of paper, a blackboard, or a slate. At worst, children may learn that working with computers is dull and uninteresting. In either case they get no idea of the tremendous potential of this new tool for solving personally interesting problems.

There are, indeed, many useful applications for computers. Open ended programs such as simulations, graphics, and micro-worlds can encourage new vistas for children (Clements 1987). Through such applications, computers offer new ways to teach old lessons and encourage children to find new ways of thinking about old problems. Through the use of technology, traditional knowledge and skills can be presented in radically different ways, thus deepening and expanding traditional curriculums. Children using PC Logo, for instance, can come to grips with some powerful mathematical ideas in new and different ways (Papert 1980).

Greta Fein (1987) gives a cogent example when she describes the awe and wonder of a group of five-year-old children who typed s-h-i-t into the computer and were able to display it in lower case as well as upper case (Fein tells us that the effect was electrifying as the children "discovered a basic orthographic principle: case does not change the sound or meaning of words." She adds, "This discovery put them a year ahead of the formal curriculum."

Technology also makes it possible for people to change how they think about problems. Lawler (1985) commented, "The mind generates new problems for itself." Technology also generates new problems for the mind. Computers, like the printing press, are revolutionizing how people think about the world. They offer new and different ways to represent ideas, a different kind of symbol system, a different way to conceptualize and manipulate data. And like print, this new way to represent thought has the potential to significantly alter our capacity to solve problems. For instance, graphic representations can be created and altered by pressing a key, thus providing rapid changes of perspective, without having to move from one's chair. Problem simulations allow the computer user to try out many different possible solutions, again, without leaving the keyboard or the mouse.

The depth and extensiveness of the computer as a tool is just being explored and we have little idea of its future uses. Schools for the most part continue to think of the content of their curriculums as if it is carved in stone. Most schools remain focused on traditional content, rather than on how to prepare children to think differently. For instance, in many early childhood programs, children are drilled on number facts without drawing on their intuitive problem-solving capabilities by using manipulatives and language (Kamii and DeClark 1984). Such programs have stressed teaching children mathematics by rote, rather than helping them see how numbers are useful in daily problem solving. Emphasis on memorization and discrete skills learned out of context inevitably plays a role in convincing children that their ability to reason has no place in mathematics, a lesson likely to impede their study of science and technology.

Technology Education For Young Children: Learning Complex Skills

What technologically relevant information and skills can young children learn by using computers? Can we use the knowledge of how children learn other complex skills, such as print literacy, to guide technology curriculum? This was done in a project conducted by myself and my colleague, Jill Bradley, at Olive Harvey Community College Child Development Center in Chicago. The purpose of this project was to give four- and five-year-old children from a poor community in Chicago an opportunity to use computers, an experience most of them were unlikely to have at home.

Two Apple IIE computers were available to the children during their free play periods and could be used to make graphics, play games, or just explore. The purpose of providing computer experience was not to teach children to program computers, but to introduce them to a new world of technology. No didactic lessons were given. Children learned the computers' attributes from interacting with them. Children's questions were answered when possible and when not, the children were encouraged to try their ideas and to see what would happen.

The goal of the project was to help children develop an overview for understanding computers and other technological tools. When children acquire complex skills, they need both an overview of the activity and the discrete bits and pieces of the structure of the activity. Thus, infants understand the purpose of communication and they learn to speak individual words. Children understand the purposes of reading and writing and they learn decoding and encoding skills. Embedded in the overview are many different contexts that give meaning to social behaviors, cognitive tasks, self and other perceptions, physical skills, and emotional states. The context directs children's attention to the relevant things to be learned and provides meaning for the separate skills and knowledge involved.

Young children learn through play. In play children project themselves into controlling roles so that they are the doers and the users of society's artifacts. This is what we see when children pretend to keep house, or be a doctor, or drive a car. Their understanding of mothering is displayed in rocking the baby, their understanding of doctoring is represented by carrying a special bag or wearing a stethoscope, and their grasp of truck driving is displayed by honking a pretend horn. It is through acting as if, playing as if, that children come to define themselves in relation to activities and other people. Projection of self into social roles opens up new vistas of understanding of the activity itself. By imitating what they have observed, children begin to understand the activity better.

Young children go through several stages when learning complex skills. First, they learn by observing and imitating what they consider to be the relevant aspects of an activity, usually the concrete and perceptual aspects of the task being performed. During this phase their overview is limited to the concrete and perceptual aspects of the task. The children in the computer project repeatedly gave us evidence in their play of how they took half-understood facts and relationships, and by playing with them, understood them better. For example, during fantasy play, one child refused another child's request saying, "I can't do it, the computer is down."

Children also must learn social roles. Many children in the Olive Harvey Center did not regularly see adults engaged in technological activities or were unaware of what the adult was doing when engaged with computers and calculators. Therefore, the children were taken on field trips to observe adults using technology. Trips to offices, grocery stores, and computer labs gave them valuable insight into adult roles and behavior. The children were also permitted to use computers, tape recorders, and calculators. By imitating their adult models, they gained additional knowledge about the attributes of the technology and the behavior of those who use it.

Gradually, as children enlarge their understanding they can perform parts of a complex skill or activity. While children may not fully understand why they do what they do, often they can become quite skilled. By the age of four, many children can turn on and tune television sets, dial grandmother on the phone, and read fast-food signs. They can do all these things without understanding the electronics that control televisions and telephones, or the symbol system that controls written language. They begin to attend to the internal structure of how things work and ask questions about it.

Children in the Child Development Program learned to use computers in this way. They turned them on, loaded the disk, and touched keys in order to achieve some end like getting letters on the screen or changing its colors. This was the time when a variety of programs were useful: games, palettes, and graphics. The children were unafraid and willing experimenters and learned about computers from their playful interaction with them.

A few of the children succeeded in "breaking the code" and were able to program the computer from some logical understanding rather than through a learned series of steps. This is comparable to the stage in reading and writing when children sound out words and invent spellings. The children understand not only what the end product will look like, but know how to get there.

There are two major skills required for children to break the code of computers. They must be able to conceptualize a problem in a particular way and direct the computer so that it accomplishes their plan. Our children did not became very proficient at programming, even using a simplified graphics program. They did understand, however, that letters and numbers were necessary ingredients to the process and would "pretend" to make graphic figures by alternately pressing letter and number keys. By age seven, a few children could program by themselves in Logo and create a predetermined graphic. All of the children, however, had a clear belief that they would "someday" be computer experts, able to make the computer do their bidding. One frequently heard chant was, "the computer is a dumb animal and you have to tell it what to do." This slogan reflected an attitude about their relationship to computers we hoped would endure.

The similarities between how children played with computers and how they pretended to read and write were unequivocal and counsel against didactic teaching of an array of computer subskills. Through playful interaction, children can gain considerable understanding of the complex social and symbolic skills intrinsic to technology.

Teacher Attitudes

Guiding young children in interactions with technological tools and encouraging constructive play with them is not an easy task. It places a heavy responsibility on teachers. Many early childhood teachers are not confident in their own ability to do mathematics and science. They are unclear about how such knowledge develops in children, and have conservative expectations for children's performance. Most early childhood teachers do not have a lot of knowledge about or experience with computers. Modems, bauds, and ikons are well outside their range of knowledge.

Some preschool and primary teachers even question the appropriateness of early emphasis on computers. Cuffaro (1984) makes a powerful case for giving top priority to the traditional materials and equipment of early childhood education—blocks, paints and crayons, dress-up clothes, and story books. It is not necessary, however, to deny the importance of these activities in order to recommend a focus on technology. In fact, many of these activities are easily combined with a technology curriculum. Exposure to technology need not be more taxing to young minds than exposure to books and dictation, and the methods for teaching can be similar (Lawler 1985).

Objectives For Early Childhood Computer Education

Observations of the computer project at the Olive Harvey Child Development Center led to the formulation of six objectives for the technological education of young children. First, children should learn that people control technology. To most adults this seems obvious. But for young children, it is not so clear. Do people control thunder? The sun? Electric lights? The toilet flush? These are salient issues for young children. Toddlers enjoy turning lights on and off and flushing the toilet, repeatedly demonstrating their control over these objects. Young children can learn to operate complex tools such as record players, televisions, tape recorders, and computers. With help and supervision, they can learn to turn them on and off, and select the programs that interest them.

Children should also learn that people actually produce the programs and records and tapes that they see and hear just as they produce books. We help children learn about books by encouraging them to handle them and to listen to stories, and to write their own stories to share with family and friends. They learn to take ideas from others and to encode their ideas to give to others. In the same way, we need to let children use technology to get ideas from others and to produce content for others. Graphics programs, micro-worlds, and computer painting are just a few examples of how young children can create personally interesting effects and problems using computer technology. Children can even participate in making audio- and video-tapes of their dramatizations, music, and reading in order to learn about this aspect of technology. Children can learn to be makers as well as users.

The second objective is for children to learn that there are different forms of technology. Just as children learn the various forms of written language—stories, poems, and nonfiction—children can learn the different forms of technology—calculators, telephones, tape recorders, and more. They need to know what these tools are good for, when and how. For instance, computers can be used to spill out what they have in them, or as containers to hold one's thoughts and ideas. Grocery clerks use computers in one way, secretaries in another, and writers in yet another. Telephones can be used to call across the hall, across town, or across the world. Different ways of using technology are available for children to observe if alert adults provide the opportunity.

The third objective is for children to learn that technology has rules that control how it works. While young children may not be able to fully understand the rules that govern the various technologies, they can begin to understand that there are rules. Just as young children grasp that clustering letters into units is a significant aspect of reading without being able to read, they can also understand that typing letters and numbers and moving the mouse are significant aspects of computer use. All young children can grasp the notion that there are procedures that must be learned and skills that must be mastered if a technological tool is to be controlled. Connecting wires for buzzers and bells, putting batteries in flashlights, and using joysticks to control robots helps children understand the importance of these rules, if adults set up situations that call them to the children's attention. Solomon and Gardner (1986) point out that children can play with LOGO and never attend to the powerful ideas if adults do not help them see its possibilities.

The fourth objective is for children to begin learning the language of technology. Children can learn the technical language that we use when we talk about computers, such as "load the disk" and "attach the modem." We have good reason to suppose that the years between four and eight are exceptionally good times to expose children to language learning. It is a time of rapid vocabulary acquisition, particularly when children have concrete experiences with the actions or processes being discussed. It is a time of intuitive rule making based on the child's interactions and understanding. Children will learn best how to talk about computers if they talk about them in context with adults in personally meaningful exchanges.

The fifth objective is for children to learn about the symbol system that underlies computers and permits them to engage the machine's potential. For instance, DOS tells you it is listening with an "A" prompt, Basic with OK; the Mac has Ikons, and Logo has a turtle. Each one uses a different symbol for the same operation. These differences sometimes frustrate adults, but children adapt easily.

One may wonder whether a new symbol system for thinking should be introduced before the other two, language and print, are fully mastered. Despite the lack of hard evidence, I believe it can be beneficial. Playing with computers may actually support and speed up children's understanding of other forms of communication. For example, as children work with print, they deepen their

126

understanding of language. Similarly, as children work with computers, they may deepen their understanding of the relationship between print, language, and computers.

The final objective is for children to begin to think about sequential problem-solving strategies. The core of learning about computers is to be able to engage the power to solve problems. Telling the computer what to do is particularly difficult for young children who can do things themselves but cannot explain clearly how they did it. Metacognition, or thinking about thinking, is to some extent a maturation-driven accomplishment but children can be helped to develop this skill by reflecting on their actions. Making flowcharts and matrix boards, writing and enacting stories, and planning and reviewing free-choice activities are all ways for children to learn the importance of thinking about thinking.

*   *   *

Technology is a tool. What we do with it, what purposes it serves, and how society handles the problems and resources that technology makes possible are decisions made by people—by us—and not determined by some inherent property of the technology itself. Solomon and Gardner (1986) wrote that "computers do not affect learners in any direct way; it is the way they are used that is crucial."

Early childhood is the time to begin thinking about and planning for children's technological education. It is the time to help children see themselves as participants in the technological revolution, as creative users of the tools of the 21st century. It is a time for children to learn through playful experimentation and real-life feedback, rather than through formal lessons. Probably the greatest limitation to technological advancement is the notion that there is one right way or one right answer to problems. To look for new ways of solving old problems, and to look for new problems to solve, are the attributes most likely to bear fruit for the children in the future. Teachers need to build opportunities into the curriculum for children to think creatively—even if the answer turns out to be wrong. Children need opportunities to think collaboratively because seeing another person's perspective may push them to higher levels of performance.

Finally, early childhood teachers need to awaken children's interest in technology through their own interest and skill. Teachers need to educate themselves about technology, and about math and science, if they, in turn, are

127

to educate young children. And this will mean joining the technological revolution.

References

Association for Supervision and Curriculum Development. (1988). "U.S. Students Given Poor Marks in Science." ASCD *Update*. 30, 8: 2.

Clements, D. (1987). "Research in Review. Computers and Young Children: A Review of Research." *Young Children* 43, 1: 34-43.

Cuffaro, Harriet. (1984). "Microcomputers in Education: Why is Earlier Better?" *Teachers College Record* 85, 4: 559-567.

Fein, G. (1987). "Technologies for the Young." *Early Childhood Research Quarterly* 2, 3:227 -243.

Kamii, C., and G. DeClark, (1984). *Young Children Reinvent Arithmetic: Implications of Piaget's Theory.* New York: Teachers College Press.

Lawler, R. (1985). *Computer Experience and Cognitive Development.* New York: John Wiley & Sons.

Maier, E. (1987). "One Point of View: Basic Mathematical Skills or School Survival Skills?" *Arithmetic Teacher* 35, 1: 2.

Papert, S. (1980). *Mindstorms. Children, Computers and Powerful Ideas.* New York: Basic Books.

Shamos, M. (1988). "The Lesson Every Child Need Not Learn." *The Sciences* 28, 4: 14-20.

Solomon, G., and H. Gardner, (1986). "The Computer as Educator: Lessons From Television Research." *Educational Researcher* 15, 1: 13-19.

Stigler, J. (1988) "Research into Practice: The Use of Verbal Explanation in Japanese and American Classrooms." *Arithmetic Teacher* 36, 2: 27-30.

17

Curriculum Development for Gender Equity in Computer Education

Kay Gilliland

*A*ll citizens need some understanding of computers to develop the intellectual skills now being influenced by computer use and to perform well in the increasing number of careers that depend on computing (Clarke 1986). Half of the working people in the United States are women, yet girls in school today generally do not believe computers will be useful to them, do not expect to like computing, and see the use of computers as a male-oriented activity (Hess and Miura 1984, Kreinberg and Stage 1983, U.S. Dept. of Labor 1983). Schools must play an active part in changing these perceptions.

In one study of school-based computer learning, girls who took a required computer course held even more negative feelings toward computers upon completing the course than did girls who had not taken the course. Boys who completed the same course were significantly more positive in their attitudes toward computers than were boys who had not taken the course (Collis 1986). Educators must develop courses to maximize computer experience for girls, develop girls' awareness of the need for computing skills, highlight the contributions of women to computing, and present opportunities for girls to learn through their strengths. These experiences should extend to mathematics and science, where females are also underrepresented.

Administrators, teachers, and other curriculum developers must find ways to design courses that will provide positive experiences for students who may not otherwise learn to use computers effectively. If girls depend on schools for such experiences, we must ensure that school courses are highly motivating. Girls *can learn* and *will need* this powerful new technology.

Inservice for Curriculum Developers

EQUALS in Computer Technology (EQTEC) is a 30-hour inservice program for administrators, teachers, and other K-12 curriculum developers who are concerned about equitable computer education in the schools. It is specifically designed to help educators plan curriculum and instruction to intervene in the pattern of computer avoidance by females and underrepresented minority students. EQUALS has served more than 10,000 California educators and 6,000 educators in 34 other states since its inception in 1977. EQUALS' mathematics workshops provide strategies and materials that encourage all students, particularly females and underrepresented minorities, to recognize the value of mathematics, enjoy the study, persist when the going gets hard, and continue in math-based fields.

Computers were always part of the EQUALS mathematics workshops, but participants requested a much more comprehensive course, with strategies for equitable computer use in all subjects. They were finding many of the same pressures against girls' computer participation in their schools as they had encountered in mathematics education. In addition, they were concerned that, without intensive staff development, the knowledgeable teachers in educational computing would be almost exclusively male, and thus the schools themselves would perpetuate the impression that computing is a male field.

Therefore, EQTEC focuses on the development of awareness, competence, and motivation through activities that are valuable to administrators and teachers and can become part of the regular classroom curriculums for students.

A First Requisite for Change

Awareness is a first requisite for change and is, therefore, an important strand throughout EQTEC training.[1] Activities that help create awareness include "Startling Statements," classroom research, software evaluation, logistics, strategies, historical landmarks, computers in careers, and role models.

Startling Statements

In "Startling Statements," participants explore the answers to such questions as:

Q: What percentage of home computer users are male?
A: 90 percent (Scientific Manpower Commission 1984)

Q: What percentage of *BYTE Magazine* subscribers are female?
A: 5 percent (*BYTE* Editorial Study)

Q: Women are 4 percent of all electrical and electronic engineers; what percent are they of the computer data entry operators?
A: 92 percent (Strober and Arnold 1984)

What becomes clear from the "Startling Statements" activity is that women are not participating in the computer revolution. Recognizing this, educators become more likely to plan curriculums aimed at motivating girls to use and enjoy computers.

Informal Classroom Research

What do individual students expect for themselves in the future? Girls feel, in general, that women are competent with computers, but that they, as individuals, are not (Chen 1986, Collis 1986). To assess attitudes toward computers by individual students, EQTEC educators ask students to write essays explaining how they will use their computers at age 30. Analysis of the answers provides great insight into student expectations. Although neither sex makes much mention of computers in the workplace, boys expect to use computers for games and finances, while girls want computers to give them money and do the housework (Kreinberg et al. 1983).

When high school computer courses are optional, boys tend to take advanced programming and machine language, whereas girls take data process-

---

[1] The off-line activities described in this article have been published in *Off and Running*. (1986). Tim Erickson. Berkeley, Calif.: Lawrence Hall of Science.

ing (California State Department of Education 1984). Students taking advanced placement examinations in computer science are 85 percent male, and their scores are considerably higher than those of girls who take the exams (3.07 and 2.36, respectively; College Entrance Examinations Board 1985). Educators in the EQTEC workshops compare these facts with their experiences by actually counting the number of boys and girls in elective computer classes in their schools and districts.

This informal classroom research has proved valuable in inservice training in three ways. First, the results are usually surprising to the teacher-researcher, bringing increased awareness of students' attitudes and actions and leading to increased commitment to effecting change. Second, the results are discussed with the students, giving them an opportunity to consider the implications of the findings. Third, the results can be combined with statewide or nationwide results to give a general picture to the local community of the problem at hand and to encourage progress toward a solution. Teachers have responded positively to the chance to do research related to their teaching (Kreinberg 1980, Lortie 1986).

Software Evaluation

Software evaluation for classroom use is an important and demanding task faced by conscientious curriculum developers. The teacher can make the computer a powerful tool for learning in almost any subject, but the software choices are many and difficult. Too often, advantaged white males are encouraged to use the computer for problem solving and programming, while females and some minorities are relegated to drill and practice. Even the drill-and-practice activities frequently have "male" titles and feature violent payoffs for correct answers (e.g., on-screen "explosions"). In evaluating programs, educators need to screen for bias, violence, and excessively aggressive competition.

Programs should be chosen to appeal to a wide variety of students, girls as well as boys, average students as well as high achievers, minorities, and those not only motivated by graphics and music but who prefer science and mathematics as well. Utility programs such as spreadsheets, database management programs, and word-processing programs can become dynamic means of presenting content. Consideration of all these issues, as well as the use of checklists that emphasize these points, help EQTEC participants sharpen their skills in the area of software review.

Logistics and Strategies for Equitable Computer Use

Careful planning for full and equitable use of the available equipment will benefit girls more than boys for the following reasons: girls experience fewer opportunities to use computers outside of schools (Clark 1986, Hess and Miura 1985, Miura 1986); when computers are scarce, boys are likely to claim most of the time (Firkin 1984); and girls are likely to self-select out of computing (Clark 1986). Awareness of these facts and plans for creating more opportunities for girls are addressed in EQTEC through discussion of logistics and strategies.

In talking with teachers and administrators, we have found that nearly every school has a different policy on computer use and nearly every computer set-up is different, whether in terms of the amount and quality of hardware available or the location of the computers in relation to the classroom.

Given a certain configuration, how can equitable computer access be assured? EQTEC participants identify the configurations with which they are most likely to be faced: one or a few computers in a classroom, computers in a media center, computers on portable carts, or computers in a lab. Participants examine suggestions for changes made by other educators, brainstorm possible additions to the list, try the strategies in classrooms, and revise in light of what they learn.

Careers, Historical Landmarks, and Role Models

"Careers" and "Historical Landmarks" are activities that highlight the widespread use of computers in the workplace and the contributions of women such as Grace Hopper and Ada Lovelace to the history of computing. In "Role Models," women and minorities from industry and commerce are invited to talk about their work and the use they make of computers. Themes tend to emerge and be repeated, as illustrated by the following quotes:

> If I had to choose one overall skill that is essential in my work, it would be problem solving. I am constantly drawing on my knowledge and experience to solve new and unexpected problems.
> —Engineer from Ford Aerospace and Communications

> I wouldn't think of wasting my company's time trying to solve a problem by myself when I knew there was someone else in the company who could help me.
> —Engineer from Bechtel Corporation

Participants discover the impact of such statements and invite role models to their schools to speak with students. In classroom discussions, the speakers frequently stress the importance of problem solving and cooperation.

Competence in Using Computers is Essential for Educators

Competence in using computers as tools for problem solving is essential for educators in many ways. The competent teacher becomes a positive role model for students. Even more important, competence gives the teacher the courage to allow all students to take turns in moving and setting up equipment, trying out new programs, and solving problems. The teacher who feels uncertainty about fixing the equipment or debugging the program is likely to depend entirely on the most knowledgeable students—usually males—for providing them with increased experience, denying opportunities to those who could benefit most.

Knowledge of the thinking and analytical skills essential to understanding computers enables the curriculum developer to design, modify, and use on-line and off-line computer activities to clarify difficult concepts. These activities are particularly needed by students who have not used computers extensively outside of school. The variety of programs in such an integrated curriculum involves several disciplines and, thus, appeals to the interests of both girls and boys.

Computer Language and Confidence

LOGO is our example language in EQTEC. It is easy to access, can be used in a variety of ways, and is perhaps the most powerful and flexible language presently available for a microcomputer. Participants use LOGO to design an alphabet and to construct "Spiro laterals," combining art, language, and mathematics in highly motivating lessons that can be used in a variety of ways within the school setting. It is not possible, or even desirable, to teach an in-depth LOGO course during a 30-hour computer equity workshop. However, participants are made aware of the resources, both print and course work, and may continue to develop their knowledge of the language.

Activities that EQTEC has found effective for building competence and confidence include "Limerick Machines," "Hardware Survival Skills," and plenty of hands-on microcomputer time. Analytical and thinking skills important for programming are addressed in "Robots," "Flipbooks," "Bubblesort," "Max/Min," and "Cooperative Logic." Certain LOGO activities are chosen because they require problem solving, are interactive with other students as well as the computer, and transfer easily to other disciplines.

Limerick Machines and Hardware Survival Skills

Too often girls attribute "failure" to their own inadequacy (Fennema and Sherman 1978) rather than recognizing the difficulty as an opportunity to "fix things" and learn. But working with a computer can encourage students in another direction. Students discover that things that do not work can be fixed; they look on the results of thinking as results that can be changed or fixed by different thinking; and they recognize that a mistake, rather than being a macro-event, is essential to the process of solving a problem (Papert 1980).

"Limerick Machines" is an off-line activity that can be used in the curriculum to develop diagnostic skills—the ability to observe a difficulty, figure out what is going on, and reason out a way of fixing it, or perhaps declare it unfixable for specific reasons. Practice in fixing the "broken" Limerick Machine, combined with fixing computer equipment and debugging LOGO programs, provides insight into the skills of diagnosis.

Flipbooks, Robots, Cooperative Logic, Bubblesort, and Max/Min.

LOGO users can practice making large procedures from small components. This is a powerful idea that can be used in many situations (Papert 1980). The "Flipbooks" activity creates the appearance of moving objects by drawing many small components only slightly differently from one another, demonstrating that large procedures can be built up from small components. The activity can be used in the math curriculum during a discussion of motion; in the art curriculum for animation, the making of motion pictures, and other moving graphic representations; and in the language arts curriculum by emphasizing the accompanying narrative. Wherever it is used, educators report that students of both sexes enjoy the experience and gain new understandings.

The LOGO language requires the user to give accurate, understandable instructions through the use of linear and angular measurement and a limited vocabulary. In preparation for using LOGO, EQTEC uses "Robots," an activity in which students work together to plan ways to direct a "human robot" to perform various tasks. They learn about instructions and conditions. Programming is limited by the machine being programmed, and the "Robot's" activity can be extended to simulate complex problems being solved by complex machines.

Female students often respond more positively to cooperative approaches than to competitive ones (Gilligan 1982, Shakeshaft 1986). EQTEC uses many cooperative activities, among them, "Cooperative Logic." In this activity (Figure 17.1), each of six people receives a slip of paper with part of the clues to a logic problem. The problem can be solved by talking about the information, using a pencil and paper or manipulatives, and reading the cards aloud, but the rules preclude showing the piece of paper to another member of the group. Each person must be responsible for his or her own part of the problem, and the solution cannot be obtained without the cooperation of all.

Figure 17.1

Cooperative Logic: "Who Has Which Computer Job?"

WHO HAS WHICH COMPUTER JOB?

These are your clues to help solve the group's problem. Read them to the group, but do not show them to anyone.

A computer programmer, a computer hardware engineer, and a technician traveled together to Ohio to install a computer in a steel mill.

Juanita and the computer programmer decided to make minor design changes in the computer installation.

WHO HAS WHICH COMPUTER JOB?

These are your cludes to help solve the group's problem. Read them to the group, but do not show them to anyone.

The engineer works with Barbara whenever possible out of respect for her knowledge of computers.

The computer programmer and the engineer both admire the skill and speed of the technician's work.

WHO HAS WHICH COMPUTER JOB?

These are your clues to help solve the group's problem. Read them to the group, but do not show them to anyone.

The people who went to Ohio to fix the computer, Barbara, Robert, and Juanita, have worked for the Dedicated Computer Company for eight years.

Barbara changed the connections which the computer programmer considered necessary.

WHO HAS WHICH COMPUTER JOB?

These are your clues to help solve the group's problem. Read them to the group, but do not show them to anyone.

The technician assisted Juanita in determining the source of a hardware bug.

Juanita, Robert and Barbara all liked math when they were in school.

WHO HAS WHICH COMPUTER JOB?

These are your clues to help solve the group's problem. Read them to the group, but do not show them to anyone.

Robert and the engineer decided to increase the memory capacity of the computer.

All three people love their work.

WHO HAS WHICH COMPUTER JOB?

These are your clues to help solve the group's problem. Read them to the group, but do nto show them to anyone.

The computer programmer, technician, and computer hardware engineer all use math in their work.

Barbara, Robert and Juanita all went out to dinner together to celebrate when they completed the installation of the computer.

Two other cooperative activities, "Max/Min" and "Bubblesort," are based on algorithms a programmer might use to solve sorting problems. In "Max/Min," the goal is to figure out what the program does and how it does it. In "Bubblesort," a group of four or five people stand in line, with the first person holding the control card. Only the person who has the control card at any time may move or cause others to move. Whenever a person gets the control card, she or he starts over. The instructions should be read aloud so the groups can understand what is happening and help out.

Bubblesort: *"Control Sheet"*

Bubblesort Control Card

START:

IS THERE someone in front of you?
 NO? then give this to the person behind you.
 YES? then go on . . .

DOES the person in front of you have a name that comes after yours in the alphabet?
 YES? then trade places with that person and go back to START:
 NO? then go on . . .

IS THERE someone behind you?
 YES? then give this to the person behind you.
 NO? whew! Then announce that the sort is done!

Evaluation

Participants evaluate the 30-hour inservice through a rating sheet for each activity, comment cards written at the end of each day, and a journal kept throughout the workshop. The ratings are generally high and the comments positive.

Participants also keep journals throughout the academic year. These journals reflect the struggles most went through to simply become familiar with the computer as a tool and develop confidence in their own skills.

One of the problems mentioned most often in the journals is the lack of time for curriculum development. Also mentioned are problems concerning what to teach at a particular time, how best to teach concepts, and how to manage time. The frequently expressed feelings of EQTEC participants echo the statements of teachers in the Second National Survey of Instructional Uses of School Computers (Becker 1985). When teachers were asked what was the most serious problem in computer use, the response "no time for the teacher to develop computer-based activities" was second only to "lack of equipment."

Nearly all journals included entries concerning gender equity and a renewed determination to ensure that girls as well as boys would benefit from the new technology.

* * *

Schools are able to make changes when teachers are excited about their work and feel empowered to make those changes. Lortie (1986) has written persuasively about the need for today's highly educated teaching force to have more autonomy and more opportunity to share practical experience and do research related to their own work. More than half of the participants in EQTEC chose to write for grants or to create workshops and inservice presentations for their own faculties. If teachers learn most from other teachers, as research indicates (Kottkamp, Provenzo, and Cohn 1986), then we must turn to teachers for help in redesigning our curriculum.

Given time and a background of information and experience, teachers will develop curriculums that maximize the computer experience for girls; develop girls' awareness of the need for computing skills; highlight the contributions of women to computing; and create opportunities for girls to learn through their strengths, persist when the going gets tough, and keep their options open for the new and demanding world they will face in the future.

References

Becker, H.J. (1985). *Second National Survey of Instructional Uses of Schools' Computers*. Baltimore, MD: Center for the Social Organization of Schools, John Hopkins University.

BYTE Editorial Study. (Aug 1983). McGraw-Hill Research.

California State Department of Education. (1984). *California Assessment Program*. Sacramento, CA.

Chen, M. (April 1986). "Gender and Computers: The Beneficial Effects of Experience on Attitudes." Paper presented at the Annual Meeting of the American Educational Research Association in San Francisco.

Clarke, V. (April 1986). "Girls and Computing: A Study of Primary Schoolchildren." Paper presented at the American Educational Research Association in San Francisco.

College Entrance Examination Board. (1985). *1985 Advanced Placement Program*. Western Regional Office, San Jose, CA.

Collis, B. (1986). "Secondary School Females and Inequities in Computer Education Experience." Paper presented at the World Congress on Education and Technology in Vancouver, B.C.

Erickson, T. (1986). *Off and Running. The Computer Offline Activities Book*. Berkeley, CA: Lawrence Hall of Science.

Fennema, E.,and J. Sherman. (1978). "Sex-related Differences in Mathematics Achievement and Related Factors: A Further Study." *Journal for Research in Mathematics Education* 9, 3: 189-203.

Firkin, J. (October 1984). *Computers in Schools*. Melbourne: VISE.

Gilligan, C. (1982). *In a Different Voice*. Cambridge: Harvard University Press.

Hess, R.D., and I.T. Miura. (Aug 1985). "Gender Differences in Enrollment in Computer Camps and Classes." *Sex Roles* 13, 3-4: 193-203.

Kottkamp, R.B., E.F. Provenzo, and M. Cohn. (April 1986). "Stability and Change in a Profession: Two Decades of Teacher Attitudes, 1964-1984." *Phi Delta Kappan* 67, 8: 559-567.

Kreinberg, N. (May 1980). "The EQUALS Program: Helping Teachers to Become Researchers and Problem Solvers." *Journal of Staff Development* 1, 1.

Kreinberg, N., and E. Stage. (1983). "EQUALS in Computer Technology." In *The Technological Woman: Interfacing with Tomorrow*, edited by J. Zimmerman. New York: Praeger.

Lortie, D.C. (April 1986). "Teacher Status in Dade County: A Case of Structural Strain?" *Phi Delta Kappan* 67, 8: 568-575.

Miura, I.T. (April 1986). "Understanding Gender Differences in Middle of School Computer Interest and Use." Paper presented to the American Educational Research Association in San Francisco.

Papert, S. (1980). *Mindstorms: Children, Computers, and Powerful Ideas.* New York: Basic Books.

Scientific Manpower Commission. (July-August 1984). *Manpower Comments.* 21, 6.

Shakeshaft, C. (March 1986). "A Gender at Risk." *Phi Delta Kappan* 67, 7: 499-503.

Strober, M.H., and C.L. Arnold. (1984). "Integrated Circuits/Segregated Labor: Women in Three Computer-related Occupations." Stanford, Calif.: Institute for Research on Educational Finance and Governance, School of Education, Stanford University.

United States Department of Labor. (December 1983). *Handbook of Labor Statistics, Bulletin 2175.*

18

Program Descriptions

Cynthia Warger

Electronic Classroom Comes of Age

Contact: William Bosher
               Henrico County Schools
               7900 Messer Road
               Richmond, VA 23231

District Background

Henrico County Public Schools is a suburban school system located outside Richmond, Virginia, that serves a diverse population of young people in 51 schools. Its students come from approximately 30 percent of the county's 79,767 households. These households are located in densely populated suburban to rural neighborhoods and represent a broad range of socioeconomic situations.

Program Mission

From the advent of an electronic classroom in 1984 to the recent opening and utilization of an on-site Instructional Television Fixed Services (ITFS) studio, the district has been building a partnership with technology to fulfill an overall mission of preparing its 31,567 students for a rapidly changing world.

Overview of the Program

Recognizing that the country was in the midst of the technological advances that futurists spoke of years ago, Henrico County Public Schools began to plan for the next generation of technology that would be essential for effective classroom instruction. In 1982-83, $135,000 of local funding served as the seed for an aggressive program in instructional and managerial technology.

142

The following year, the school system obtained $170,000 in federal funds through the Chapter II program for instructional technology. Also in 1983-84, $400,000 of county funds were set aside for staff development. Included in that funding was a major commitment to computer training for teachers. The district realized that teachers must understand and be comfortable with technology before it could become an effective teaching tool.

In the fall of 1984, the Virginia General Assembly appropriated more than $3 million to establish the Governor's Center for Educational Innovation and Technology. Varina High School in eastern Henrico County was selected as the site of the project that tested, in practice, educational initiatives to strengthen instruction and administration through technology applications, the restructuring of decision making, and programs that gave students support in every area of campus life.

In the initial funding for the project, which became known as the Varina Project because of its location, approximately $250,000 was used to cover start-up costs of a studio and control room to serve an electronic classroom. Additional funding was provided to school divisions interested in participating in the form of a one-time grant for the purchase of a television monitor, video cassette recorder, a toll-free telephone number, and an antenna for reception. After the first year, the state charged participating school divisions $245 per student per class. Henrico students are exempt from the fee because facilities are furnished and operations are administered by the school division.

The Electronic Classroom

The electronic classroom was established as, and remains, a partnership with the Virginia Department of Education. It offers classes to students in small, rural school divisions that their own schools are unable to provide. Advanced placement calculus and English, as well as Latin I and Latin II are taught.

The first classes were broadcast in January 1985 to 84 students in nine school divisions. During the 1987-88 school year, there were 335 participating students in 31 school divisions, not including the students on-site at Varina.

From the Varina High School campus, a microwave signal takes the broadcast to the studios of WCVE, Central Virginia's educational television station, where classes are then broadcast on the station's Channel 57. In 1989, several of the classes also went out via satellite.

A key factor in this program's success has been the interactive feature of the classroom. Through a preprogrammed toll-free telephone number, students at receive sites are able to talk to the instructor during the live broadcasts and answer questions. The Varina on-site students, as well as every receiving student, can hear this discussion through televisions. In a very short time, the electronic classroom teacher is just as much a part of the students' educational experience as one of the teachers at their school.

Throughout the year, special events are planned so that electronic classroom teachers may get to know the satellite students and so that the students have the opportunity to meet each other. An orientation program has been held at Varina at the end of the first week of school to set course expectations. A Christmas social has been held at Varina with time allotted for discussion of the semester exam. A spring picnic gives students an opportunity to exchange information and talk about their college choices, and gives the teacher an opportunity to talk with them about taking the standardized advanced placement tests.

Since the electronic classroom teachers carry a full student load, they are required to teach only one class each day. They are scheduled for three hours of preparation for the broadcast, two hours of telephone time for satellite students to call in with questions, and one hour of duty period. Most student work and papers are graded by the electronic classroom teacher, but part-time teachers are being used for assignments and grading aids as enrollments increase. Assignments and papers are currently sent through the mail, but research is being done on moving to facsimile and computer transfer of print materials and tests.

Program Evaluation

Increasing enrollment attests to the popularity of the classes, and superintendents of receiving divisions, citing the expanded curriculum their schools are able to offer, have commended the program. The most important assessment, however, is the performance of the students who enrolled in the classes. In standardized testing, students who have participated in the electronic classroom have shown positive results, with the majority scoring as well or better than the national average on advanced placement testing.

Because the classes are broadcast on public television, an interesting and unanticipated audience has developed. While no research has been done to determine how large the adult audience may be, several senior citizens have written, and teachers are often recognized by members of the general public. One nursing home resident in northern Virginia wrote to request a workbook so that she could cover lessons when television reception was not good. A live television broadcast from the classroom has enabled citizens to phone in questions to the superintendent and school board members. Other uses have included making instructional videotapes for the Students Understanding Neighbors (SUN) elementary foreign language program; broadcasting GED classes to adults and prison inmates in Central Virginia through an ITFS system utilizing one-way video, and two-way audio capabilities; and a closed-circuit television distribution system in use on the Varina High School Campus.

Cultural Awareness Programs

The SUN Foreign Cultures/Languages program began in 1985 with a grant from the Virginia Department of Education, which provided funding for a pilot study to be conducted from 1985 to 1992. The program is intended to provide opportunities for all elementary school children to develop a cultural awareness and social understanding of other countries and their languages.

Through the use of an instructional videotape package, the SUN program compares and contrasts Canada and Mexico to the United States. The package's three major components consist of: (1) a detailed manual with a written script, content analysis, objectives, vocabulary, pronunciation guide, games, songs, and art activities; (2) a complete set of audio tapes to assist teachers and students in practicing vocabulary and songs for each lesson; and (3) a complete 150-minute videotape that includes the dramatization and television instruction for 24 lessons, complete with props native to the country, costumes indicative of content, games, music for the lesson's objectives, and the drill and practice of vocabulary that is introduced in each lesson.

The SUN videotape bridges the gap between an elementary teacher who has never had a foreign language and a fully certified secondary language teacher who is unfamiliar with teaching strategies for elementary students. French and Spanish teachers from Henrico's middle and high schools appear on the television tapes that are shown to elementary students from the county.

Future of the Program

In the seven years since initial funding for technology, a department of technology has been established and objectives have been set to assure that technology would serve as a medium to strengthen education, that utilization rather than acquisition would remain the most important factor. Among the objectives are:

- Assuring that all students are computer literate before high school graduation,
- Improving instructional effectiveness through the correct applications of instructional computing technology and software,

- Providing telemedia production/dissemination services to improve instruction and staff development, and
- Providing media resources and training to the staffs of central administration and school sites.

Today, there are 1700 microcomputers in the schools. Their use is based on the premise that computers should serve as a tutor and a tool. Technology should empower educators to more effectively and efficiently perform the tasks they are already required to perform. This philosophy can be applied to the teaching of mathematics where skills and concepts can be learned in a shorter amount of time with the use of computers. The time saved is used to teach mathematics applications.

Computers serve as tools when they help teach students skills such as word processing and the compilation of databases and spreadsheets as well as communications and graphics. While all of these programs are currently conducted at various Henrico Schools, they are not necessarily in every school. For example, language arts programs are used at the kindergarten and first-grade level to help begin teaching written language skills, but are offered only at schools where early language skills are most needed.

Another feature of Henrico's quest for state-of-the-art technology applications occurred last year when six students participated in an International Cultural Exchange sponsored and financed by McGraw-Hill and Tandy Corporation. The program enabled students to transmit messages to a host computer in Minnesota that served as the center for the foreign message exchange activity. Students from schools in Japan, Australia, Mexico, Argentina, Kenya, Italy, West Germany, and Switzerland exchanged information about everything from the area in which they live to the amount of time and type of labor required to buy a hamburger. The program is being replicated at a middle school this year (again courtesy of Tandy and McGraw-Hill), and plans are underway to make this technological communications link available at each middle and high school.

Other highlights of Henrico's applications of technology include:

- Retrospective conversion of library resources from card catalogs to computers that allows students at each school to access information from a computer terminal that includes entries from public libraries, (A delivery system moves requested materials between schools. The system saves the costs of duplicating expensive resource material and increases the resources available to students.) '
- Electronic mail system using a mainframe and personal computers, (The system allows immediate, simultaneous information transmission

146

between schools and the central office while greatly reducing the "paper" handling formerly required.)

- An asynchronous communications typesetting system to transmit copy for student and community newsletters to the central office for professional typesetting,
- Desktop publishing with a MacIntosh II that allows the Public Information Office to efficiently write, edit, and design publications, (The system has increased quality and volume, both necessary to meet school division and public information needs.)
- Computerized student, personnel, and financial records, and
- School Board update through which board members receive a weekly videotape that decreases the reading time required for school-related materials. (The program has been well received, and has also allowed for visual introductions to various central administrative offices for new members.)

Under the premise that most of what educators are required to know can be learned via television viewing in each local school, thus conserving time and gasoline, ongoing assessments of informational procedures such as staff development are being made. At the same time, close attention is being given to maintaining the human, interpersonal contact, and communication that television cannot replace.

While balancing what is presented on a screen versus what is presented face-to-face, Henrico continues to look to the future, planning for single-purpose items such as word processors and typewriters with printers. The schools plan in 1990 to implement a keyboarding pilot at the third-grade level using a single-purpose device. At $40 per keyboard, such devices can be extremely economical compared to the overall costs for multi-purpose microcomputers. Henrico Schools constantly explores new technological innovations, but only implements them throughout the county when there is concrete evidence that such innovations will work to make the schools and their management more effective and efficient.

In 1988, Henrico Schools was the first public school system in Virginia to win a U.S. Senate Productivity Award; an award that honors organizations for productivity and quality improvement efforts. While the electronic classroom was instrumental in the selection process, it was not the sole determining factor. The school division's commitment to preparing students for today's and tomorrow's world reaches far beyond one single program.

Technology for Access, Productivity, and Achievement

Contact: Harvey Barnett, Director of Technology Support
Cupertino-Fremont Model Technology Schools
10300 North Blaney Avenue
Cupertino, CA 95014
(408) 252-3000 x481

District Background

The Cupertino Union School District—a suburban district with eight
nationally recognized and/or state-distinguished schools—serves close to
11,400 students in a 26-square mile area that includes the City of Cupertino
and portions of five other cities in the center of California's Silicon Valley. The
district contains 18 K-6 elementary schools and four 7th and 8th grade junior
high schools, including two alternative schools.

The district's large size provides for considerable diversity. Our students
speak 23 different languages. Some 1,000 students with learning disabilities or
physical limitations receive special education services; more than 2,000 students participate in an extended learning program under funding from the
state's Gifted and Talented Education Program; a large number of our students
are non- or limited-English speaking; several schools receive federal Chapter 1
funds; a significant number of families receive Aid for Dependent Children
monies; and the student turnover rate approaches 40 percent in some schools.

District test scores rank in the top three percent of the states's public
schools (top 10 percent nationwide), and all our students reflect the high expectations their parents—and we—hold for their personal and educational success.

Program Mission

The central vision for the district's K-8 technology program is based on
the belief that the teacher is the primary vehicle for instruction and is, therefore, the key to implementing changes in the classroom. Teachers, when
provided direct and appropriate access to the tools and resources of technology,
develop, evaluate, and disseminate an instructional delivery model that uses
technology across all curriculum areas and grade levels. Because change is a
process, not an event, ongoing staff development and support are essential for
successful implementation of technology-enhanced instruction.

To cement the change process, the Board of Education adopted, in
December 1986, a long-range strategic plan that set the stage for a truly innovative exploration. One of the major goals of the Cupertino Union School

148

District's "Strategic Plan: 1986-2000" is to use instructional technology effectively. In support of this goal, the objectives of the strategic plan have been designed to provide access for teachers, students, and administrators to the tools required for efficient, effective technology use.

Overview of the Program

Instructionally, technology is to be used as an additional tool to motivate students, to reinforce and reteach concepts, and to foster cooperative learning and collaboration. Further, the district is committed to piloting new and promising technologies and programs, several of which are presently being implemented. The district has purchased 17 Apple computers for each K-6 elementary school computer lab. Providing each elementary classroom with a teacher technology station containing a computer, printer, large screen monitor, and VCR is a primary objective of the technology plan.

Helping teachers to increase their comfort level with technology is inherent to the attainment of district goals. An ambitious, ongoing staff development program combined with teacher access to technology is the key to effective use of the technology in the labs and classrooms.

Technology Lead Teacher Network. The use of technology in Cupertino classrooms had its beginning a decade ago when several teachers in isolated classrooms piloted activities exploring instructional and personal uses of computers. The fledgling experiment was funded by a federal grant. The teachers also started an informal network, not unlike a user's group. They met regularly and shared their successes and frustrations. From these grass roots beginnings, the district recognized the value of computers as instructional tools, developed labs at each school site, and offered staff development classes and training for teachers.

Today's "Technology Lead Teacher Network" grew out of that informal user's group. The Lead Teacher Network now has one teacher representative from each school in the district, and is chaired by a technology mentor teacher. The group still shares their technology experiences. In addition, they present model lessons, host guest speakers on new and emerging technologies, explore curriculum integration and often make recommendations to the administration about technology issues. The lead teachers then disseminate the information to the other teachers at their schools.

The Cupertino Concept. Several years ago, the "Cupertino Concept" was developed. It is a process by which a school or district can plan and implement a technology program. The Cupertino Concept was selected as a National

Diffusion Network (NDN) project and has been adopted by numerous districts across the country.

The first district computer curriculum was an outgrowth of the Cupertino Concept. The curriculum addressed computer literacy and taught programming concepts using BASIC and Logo languages. As educational software became more readily available, the curriculum was expanded to incorporate its use. Housing the computers in a computer lab provided student access and emphasized student use.

The labs were staffed by computer aides, and classes were scheduled to go to the lab at regularly assigned times on a rotating basis. Often little or no correlation existed between the classroom curriculum and the activities in the computer lab. Student access to computers increased but teacher access did not. Computers were seen as an add-on to the curriculum, not as an integrated part of the instructional program. Students were taught computer use as a skill that was an end in itself.

Our experiments, however, demonstrated that for technology to be effective as a teaching and learning tool, it must be integrated into the curriculum. It became the philosophy of the district to use technology-assisted instruction, not technology-based instruction. In order to do that, we empower teachers by providing direct and appropriate training and access. Simulations for problem solving, word processors for writing, independent practice for math and language, and ITV for hands-on demonstrations in science are but a few of the ways teachers can use technology tools to enhance learning.

Summer Technology Institute. To address the need for teacher training, the district has, for the past two summers, conducted a Summer Technology Institute—a four-day institute that is held in August, just prior to the start of school. The presenters are mentor teachers and other Cupertino teachers who have exemplary programs in their classrooms.

Teachers who participate in the training receive either an Apple IIGS computer system for use in their classroom or a large-screen monitor and VCR. These teachers also agree to take 10 hours of follow-up training during the next school year. The Institute has been a highly successful training model for teachers and administrators.

The first year of the Institute, the principal, the lead teacher, and one other teacher from each school attended. Principals must be included in the training if they are to be effective instructional leaders. The second summer, 15 percent of each staff who had not previously attended were selected to participate. In addition, previous participants returned for one day and, in conjunction with newly trained teachers, developed a site-level technology plan.

The goal of the Technology Institute is to have all Cupertino teachers trained by 1993.

Pilot Projects. The Cupertino Union School District's commitment to exploring new and promising technologies has brought several pilot projects into the district. Three examples are the Apple Classroom of Tomorrow, the California Model Technology Schools Project, and the Nimitz/Apple Partnership. Each of these pilots explores different aspects of technology use in the classroom.

The Apple Classroom of Tomorrow (ACOT) at Stevens Creek School is a research partnership with Apple Computer, Inc. Through this program, 1st, 2nd, and 3rd grade students and their teachers have a high degree of access to technology. Keyboarding, word processing, problem-solving software, tutorials, simulations, and programs for guided and independent practice are all a part of each student's day. The ACOT model has shown us that effective keyboarding can be taught at an early age. Third grade teachers are exploring the most effective uses of home computers, as well as parent training models. Students in the ACOT classes are highly motivated. Teachers have observed that the technology helps students become better writers and problem solvers. The students' willingness to take responsibility for their own learning is seen as a major strength of the ACOT project.

The Model Technology Schools Project (MTS) is designed to examine the changing role of teachers as they integrate technology into the design, planning, implementation, and evaluation of the classroom instructional program. A joint project of the Cupertino Union School District and the Fremont Union High School District, MTS includes a high school and a feeder elementary and junior high school. The goals of the project are to:

- Demonstrate instructional use that supports state curriculum and instructional objectives,
- Develop models for training teachers and administrators,
- Support and disseminate research on instructional, administrative, and home-school uses of technology,
- Determine facility standards required for using computer, video, and interactive technologies in both new and existing schools, and
- Disseminate results of the project to decision makers and other educators.

The partnership between Nimitz School and Apple Computer, Inc., pairs corporate volunteer tutors with students in the classroom. The ongoing partnership is but one example of how technology matches schools to community resources, thus eliminating the barriers often found in educational institutions.

151

In addition to the classroom computers, plans are underway to provide each school with a Guided Learning Center (GLC). Computer activities will be located in the GLC, along with scarce technologies such as video disc players, camcorders, and multimedia stations. The GLC will also house a teacher technology center for teacher productivity and a publishing center for teacher and student use.

Each school is equipped with an antenna for instructional television reception and with the capability for downloading from the country's Instructional Television Fixed Services system. We have learned that instructional television is an effective teaching tool when it can be integrated into both the curriculum and the classroom schedule. By recording programs from ITFS, teachers can use them at times that are most appropriate to their lessons.

At the district level, the programs are administered by the Director of Technology Support under the supervision of the Associate Superintendent of Instruction. Each school is required to develop a Technology Support Plan in conjunction with the School Plan. Site level supervision is the responsibility of the principal.

Program Evaluation

Because each school has its own local "Technology Support Plan," the evaluation of the program is a local issue. Principals and school staffs collect empirical data from teacher observations along with parent and student questionnaires, and teacher evaluations.

The district continuously evaluates the various pilot programs to ensure that they are meeting their stated objectives. Programs that fulfill their promise are expanded to other schools.

Teacher attitudes have changed a great deal in Cupertino as a direct result of the technology program. As recently as two years ago, some teachers were unwilling to accept student work done on a word processor. Now some of those same teachers have a computer in their classroom. Many more teachers than can be accommodated volunteer to attend the Extended-Year Technology Institute. And several teachers who attended the institute have written grants to acquire additional technology to expand its use within the classroom instructional program.

Strongest Feature of the Program

Staff training is the strongest feature of the Cupertino program. The Extended Year Technology Institute, combined with classes offered through our staff development catalog, are the backbone of the technology training program for teachers. A very important factor of the staff development program is that almost all training is provided by district teachers including the three technology mentor teachers, the lead teachers, and others who have expertise in the use of technology.

A second critical factor that makes the staff development program strong is that it is teacher-driven. Course offerings are determined through needs assessments, and teachers feel ownership in the system.

Future of the Program

As technology evolves, the key focus for educators must be to determine the effects of technology on instructional practices and student learning—*not* on the widespread use of technology for its own sake. An equally important focus should be on developing the interactive aspects of technology. The benefits of this interactive technology should be judged on its effectiveness at increasing content learning and enhancing students' abilities to apply that content to problem solving, decision making, and communications situations.

Our concept of the Guided Learning Center is the vehicle through which we hope to restructure the way we look at the delivery of instruction. The GLC will afford us the opportunity to provide new and different resources— technology being one such resource—to improve the teaching/learning environment.

Computer-Assisted Instruction in the Classroom

Contact: Eugene Hertze, Superintendent
Central Kitsap School District
P.O. Box 8
Silverdale, WA 98383
(206) 692-4997

District Background

The Central Kitsap School District is located in a rural area that is rapidly becoming suburban. Located on the Kitsap Peninsula, approximately one hour west of Seattle by ferry and freeway, the school district has grown steadily since the construction of Trident Submarine Base within the school district. The district also serves families from the Puget Sound Naval Shipyard and the Naval Underseas Warfare Engineering Station. Approximately 70 percent of the students' families are connected with the Navy; approximately 27 percent are active-duty military personnel dependents, and the remainder are children of civil service employees or defense contractors. Transiency among the student population is extremely high.

Parents in the district are well educated and technology oriented with high expectations for schools. The community consistently supports bond issues and special levies for instructional programs. The district spends at the state average for instruction and has emphasized technology very heavily during the past five years. Currently there is approximately one instructional computer for every eleven students in the district. Instruction on computers begins in the first grade and continues through high school.

Background of the Program

Integrating technology into regular instructional programs began in 1984, when a District Task Force on Excellence made the following recommendations:

> The district should create a plan to integrate the application of technological innovation and the study of technological implication into appropriate courses across the curriculum. The district should integrate computers as a teaching tool into all appropriate classrooms. By doing so, the use of computers will assist the teacher in individualizing student education by providing the following services:

a. Determining the appropriate level of work for each student,
b. Monitoring individual student progress,
c. Providing immediate feedback to the teacher within an individualized program, and
d. Freeing teachers to work with students in more areas best served by direct human interaction.

Following that charge, the District's Computer Committee began to search for software appropriate to that purpose. During the 1985-86 school year, the committee developed guidelines for selecting a computer-assisted instruction program (CAI) for the district's newest junior high school and subsequently for an elementary school. The committee followed a nine-step process in the selection of the CAI system:

1. Review of the literature
2. Research of advertising
3. Developing educational criteria
4. In-district demonstrations
5. Site visits
6. Completing a report matrix
7. Weighing of criteria
8. Evaluation of criteria and reports
9. Selection of the system

The committee gathered information regarding what was happening in the field of computer-aided instruction and researched the advertising material of all the companies that appeared to have the potential for supplying the CAI system for the district. The committee then developed the following educational guidelines for selection of the system:

1. Hardware should be secondary to quality course software programs.
2. Courseware should deliver curriculum for kindergarten through grade 12.
3. Software should be more than simply drill and practice. It should incorporate higher-level thinking skills. And it must be easy for the educational staff to modify.
4. Software development should be ongoing and the courseware updated often.
5. Staff development and a strong inservice program must be provided by the CAI supplier.
6. The hardware and courseware should be available at a reasonable cost.

7. The program should include instruction, testing, and recordkeeping.

8. The courseware and hardware should be compatible with other ware.

9. The CAI system should be capable of supplanting, not merely supplementing, existing programs.

In addition, more specific criteria addressed features that were seen as desirable:

1. Networking should be possible both within the school and to sites at adjacent schools.

2. Interactive video programs should be operable with the system.

3. An auditory component should be available for beginning reading.

4. Other software programs should be compatible.

5. The system should be functional with varying degrees of teacher involvement.

6. Multiple printer options should be available.

7. Hardware should be compatible with other hardware existing in the district.

8. Enhancements to the CAI system should be provided to the district without extra charge.

Later in the selection process other questions evolved: Are there hidden costs? inservice costs after the initial few days? daily consultant help? supplies available on the open market? Additional questions included: Does the company have a users network organized through an electronic bulletin board or through user meetings? Is the company expanding the offering of programs — particularly at the secondary level and in foreign languages? Is the company expanding its compatibility with other software and hardware?

With these criteria and questions in mind, the committee reviewed all proposals, arranged in-district demonstrations, and made site visits to the companies' headquarters or to a school that was piloting the system.

Each committee member completed a report matrix, and subsequently the committee recommended to the Superintendent and Board of Directors that the WICAT system be obtained for the junior high school and that the Educational Systems Corporation (ESC) be selected for the elementary program. Currently, both CAI systems operate 32 stand-alone computers networked to a central computer that retains student records and the basic curriculum. Courseware purchased with the WICAT system included reading, language arts, math skills in grades K-8, algebra I & II, geometry, and French. The ESC system included 1,800 lessons in reading and mathematics K-6. A writing component has since been added.

About the Programs

Both companies provided inservice staff development sessions for the teachers for two days prior to the opening of school and then on a periodic basis throughout the school year. The cost of each program was nearly the same—approximately $120,000 including the full-time laboratory aide, appropriate classroom furniture, and the necessary electrical changes in the classrooms.

While the WICAT system was originally a closed system, the WICAT courseware can now be used with computers from any major hardware supplier. The district used MS-DOS compatible Tandy 1000s in each ESC elementary lab. Thirty-two stations are networked to a central file server, a Tandy 3000 with a CD-ROM drive.

In both systems, lessons appropriate to each student's skill level are downloaded to his/her own computer. The students are allowed to progress through the lessons at their own pace. Many of the functions of the teacher's workbooks and textbooks are combined in the interactive software, which provides students with instruction, guided practice, and independent practice on the machines as well as evaluation. Teachers can track students' progress on individual reports or with reports reflecting the entire class' work. The teacher is able to determine what the students need, and the laboratory aide does the necessary programming.

In addition to using the CAI system as sequenced, the teachers also use it in the following ways:

1. By using the diagnostic test, the teacher can identify gaps in a specific student's learning skills.

2. By assigning students specific segments to review deficient skills in order to gain mastery.

3. By selecting enrichment activities for high-ability students.

4. By generating reports of unit test results that can be shared with parents in parent-teacher conferences.

Because there is almost 90 percent compatibility of the CAI systems' objectives and the district's specific learning objectives, the testing and recordkeeping of the district's SLOs can be done via the computer, with immediate feedback to the teacher.

Students at both the junior high and elementary levels spend 25 minutes every other day in the CAI lab. Teachers also have the option of cooperating with another teacher in sending only half their students at a time to the lab.

This allows each teacher to meet with a much smaller group of students for more individualized instruction.

Evaluation

Because district testing procedures are more exact at the elementary school level, evaluation of the elementary school program has been most complete. Achievement expectations were set and an assessment design was developed. The assessment design included student achievement and student, staff, and parent attitude surveys.

Increased achievement scores were the result of excellent classroom teaching techniques practiced along with the application of correct methods of monitoring, diagnosing, and prescribing lessons through the microcomputer lab.

Parent Surveys. While the student and staff surveys were very supportive, it was important to the district to determine parent support. Parents responded to the following statements:

1. Computer-assisted instruction is valuable to my child's elementary education.
2. My student(s) likes working on computers at school.
3. I am supportive of the CAI program being used at my school.
4. Computer-assisted instruction is helpful in developing math, reading, and language arts skills for my child(ren).

Eighty-three percent of the parents felt computer-assisted instruction is valuable to the education of their child. Likewise, 92 percent of the parents responded that their student(s) like working on computers at school. Ninety-eight percent of the parents were supportive of the CAI program, and 96 percent agreed that the CAI program helped their students gain in math, reading, and language art skills. It is also interesting to note that when elementary school boundary lines were being changed, the most vocal parents were those with students scheduled to be transferred from a school having a CAI lab to a school that did not.

Another measure of parent support is the district's community schools program that used the laboratories after hours. Additional instruction is provided for children and parents who wish either enrichment or remediation. The parents pay minimal tuition to bring children for the additional instruction. The classes are conducted by laboratory aides who help the children get started in a program, work with parents, and maintain and operate the computer systems. Particular instructional problems are referred through the aide to a teacher

158

who is hired on a consulting basis to advise on placement. The program casts the computer lab aides in new roles for supporting formal instruction for students on the systems. This popular program has rapidly expanded and provides a supplement for eager learners.

Teacher reports. Teachers found that students approach long problem-solving assignments associated with higher-level thinking skills with less apprehension since working with the ESC system. There are no discipline problems in the lab. Teachers also state the maximum effectiveness of the CAI lab depends on the efficient manipulation of the program by the teacher.

Looking Ahead

As a result of the initial experience with CAI systems at one elementary school, the CAI labs have been expanded into three additional elementary schools and one additional junior high school. Plans are to add at least one system per year until all elementary schools have a CAI lab. All new buildings have a CAI lab as part of their basic equipment list.

The use of the CAI labs are not the only uses of technology in the regular instructional program in Central Kitsap School District. In addition, all schools in the district have an Apple lab for teacher use on a sign-up basis.

Technology-Based Educational and Management Programs

Contact: Arvid E. Nelson, Superintendent
Indian Springs School District No. 109
80th Street and 82nd Avenue
Justice, IL 60458

District Background

Indian Springs School District #109, an elementary school district located in southwest Cook County in the Chicago, Illinois, suburbs, serves 2,300 students in grades K-8 in five buildings.

Each year, the district receives a number of students from surrounding suburbs. From 1985 to 1988, 34 percent of the newly enrolled students came from Chicago Public Schools. During the past 15 years, the minority population of the district has increased from 2 to 15 percent. In the Indian Springs district #109, 14 percent of the students are from low-income families, and 25 percent of the children are from single-parent families. In September, 1988, 10 percent of the parents of students enrolled reported that neither parent was employed. The district experiences a very high student mobility rate that ranges from 14 to 18 percent per year.

Program Background

Certain benchmarks and milestones mark a decade of progress in implementing the technology-based educational and management programs that exist in Indian Springs District #109 today. Since 1980, the Board of Education, administrative, and teaching staff have been working together to attain the appropriate hardware and software and to develop the "peopleware" to implement the technology-based educational and management programs.

Approximately 130 microcomputers with color monitors, 256K, double disk drives, and printers have been installed in every classroom in the district, including all full-day kindergarten and self-contained special education classrooms. Each computer has approximately 30 feet of cord attached to it, so it can be moved from place to place in the classroom. During the 1985-86 school year, all six school buildings, including the Early Childhood Center, were wired, and administrative software was developed to network all of the microcomputers in each classroom to the mainframe computer located in the Central Office Complex.

The district developed funding partnerships with the Illinois State Board of Education, IBM Corporation, the United States Department of Education, and several Chicago area colleges and universities. A summary of the results of these partnerships follows.

Computer-Assisted Management Systems

During the fiscal years of 1980-81 and 1981-82, the district received approximately $85,000 from the Illinois State Board of Education through the Title IV C Program to develop and implement the project known as *Computer-Assisted Management Systems (CAMS)*. At that time, an IBM mainframe computer was installed, along with CRT units and off-site printers in all elementary schools. These were connected to the mainframe computer in the Central Office Complex by dedicated teleline. During the past nine years, very sophisticated database programs in budget and finance; student records (including health, dental, achievement test scores, and attendance); and special education (including individual educational plans for each student) have been developed by the Director of Computer Services.

Teacher Training Center

In 1983, IBM Corporation contracted with the district to become one of 30 teacher training centers established by IBM Corporation in the United States. During the past five years, the staff of Indian Springs, assisted by professors from local Chicago State University, Governors State University, and Moraine Valley Community Colleges, have offered 78 graduate courses related to the use of microcomputers in education. Since 1983, over 1,200 teachers and administrators who reside in the Chicago area have enrolled in these graduate courses.

Computer-Assisted Network Systems

In 1985, a proposal entitled *Computer-Assisted Network Systems—Establishing the Telecommunications Link Between the Teacher, the Principal, and the Office of the Superintendent (PROJECT CANS)* was funded by the United States Department of Education in the amount of $80,000. The main goal of PROJECT CANS was to provide classroom teachers with up-to-date and accurate information about their students. In many districts, much of the information in cumulative folders is neither organized nor up-to-date.

The implementation of PROJECT CANS mandated that every teacher learn how to use microcomputers in two ways: first, to assist them in the daily instructional process with their students, and, second, to assist them with administrative recordkeeping tasks.

PROJECT CANS was developed from a model that includes:

- Computer-Assisted Instruction — each classroom teacher using supplementary software on stand-alone IBM microcomputers and large screen television monitors (off-line) to assist with the instructional process,
- Computer Management of Instruction — administrative software for entering and retrieving test data, particularly in the areas of reading and mathematics, and,
- Computer Management of Classroom Activities — administrative software for entering and retrieving attendance records, grade reporting, lesson planning, general identification of information about students, health and dental records, and past achievement test scores.

This system also allows teachers to accept electronic mail, to view the daily calendar of events for the entire district, and to access their own personnel records from the mainframe computer located in the Central Office Complex.

To assist the teaching and administrative staff with the implementation of PROJECT CANS, the Curriculum/Technology Coordinating Council was established in 1987. Five full-time supervisors were employed in the following areas: computer-assisted instruction, reading/language arts, mathematics, science, and social studies. In addition, three teachers from each elementary school were selected to become team leaders to work with the subject area supervisors. In using technology in curriculum delivery, it is the responsibility of the team leaders, who represent all schools and grade levels, to accomplish the following:

- To exhibit an interest and commitment in the use of the microcomputer and other technologies in the classroom,
- To be available to attend after-school meetings for inservice training, particularly on the use of new software for CAI as well as for training on the retrieval and input modes, and
- To familiarize staff members, in their particular school buildings, with the software and work with subject area supervisors on software evaluation.

Reading Improvement

In 1986, the Reading Improvement Funds provided by Senate Bill 730 were used, along with another grant from IBM Corporation, to establish a "Writing to Read" laboratory in each individual attendance center for all kindergarten and 1st grade students. Each laboratory contains approximately nine microcomputers. In September, 1986, a microcomputer with a CD-ROM and Grolier's Electronic Encyclopedia was installed in each of the district's libraries, with accompanying teacher training.

Recent Developments

During the past four years, the district has acquired all of the Computer Research Systems Software, the IBM Basic Skills Software, and approximately 150 various pieces of instructional software for all grade levels and subject areas. All teachers employed throughout the district have access to the instructional software, and they use their microcomputers and large screen television monitors as teaching tools for every academic subject. To assist teachers with the integration of CAI into regular, daily classroom activities, especially for larger groups of students, 25-inch Zenith television monitors have been connected to the classroom microcomputers and installed in all classrooms throughout the district. These monitors have been placed on 54- and/or 44-inch Bredford carts, depending on the grade level, which allows for superb viewing and for student involvement in the instructional process. Members of the administrative and teaching staffs are in the process of developing the electronic omni for each classroom, which does and/or will include an on-line microcomputer, large-screen television monitor, interactive video disc, VCR, and CD-ROM to be installed in all classrooms within the next three to five years.

Intensive Phonics, a software program that can be operated on an IBM microcomputer, has been installed in all special education classrooms. *Intensive Phonics*, a concise, step-by-step systematic approach used to teach phonics, was developed particularly for students who need remedial programs. Special education teachers also use the *Woodcock-Johnson Compuscore Software Program*, which automates the scoring procedure for the Woodcock-Johnson Psycho-Educational Battery. This software program streamlines the process of converting raw scores obtained while administering the Woodcock-Johnson into meaningful derived scores.

In 1988, three video disc players and several laserdiscs for teaching science and mathematics were purchased. Junior high science teachers are using the science laserdiscs to introduce topics in chemistry, biology, and earth science. The mathematics laserdiscs have been used to teach the concepts of fractions, decimals, percentages, and ratios.

Program Evaluation

During the past eight years, Indian Springs District #109 has been featured in state, national, and international publications, including the *Chicago Tribune*, *New York Times*, and *Viewpoint*, in December 1981; *Illinois Project for School Reform*, in November, 1984; *Sphinx*, in July, 1985; *Education USA*, in May, 1986; *Electronic Education*, in September, 1986; *American School and University*, in February, 1987; *American School Board Journal*, July and October, 1987; and *The Executive Educator*, in July 1987. In the past eight years, the Board of Education, the administration, and the teaching staff have hosted several seminars and demonstrations and have given presentations to national and state organizations in the United States, Canada, and the Orient. In September, 1987, Indian Springs District #109 became the first public district to host a site visit for the National School Boards Association Institute for the Transfer of Technology to Education.

To date, Indian Springs District #109 has implemented a completely computerized system that provides for computer-assisted telecommunications to transmit management information of all types between the Central Office Complex and the classrooms located in the various elementary and junior high schools. The district represents an example of what the applications of computer technology can establish for teachers, students, and administrators. The district exemplifies a cooperative effort between the local and state education agencies, institutions of higher learning, and a private corporation.

Indian Springs District #109 has become a lighthouse district for other districts to follow as they develop their plans for incorporating technology into their school programs. Indian Springs provides one model of how a district can explore alternatives to meet the individual needs of students who will live and work in the information age of the 21st century.

A District Model for Technology

Contact: Barbara Strobert, Principal
Montclair Public Schools
Watchung School
14 Garden Street
Montclair, NJ 07042
201-783-8974

District Background

Montclair, New Jersey, is a culturally and economically diverse community of 39,000 residents located a few miles west of New York City. The school system enrolls 5,100 students, of whom 49 percent are minority (predominately black), in six elementary schools, two middle schools, and one high school. The community prides itself on both its outstanding record of academic achievement and its commitment to equity in education. With all of its schools designated as magnets, Montclair is truly a system of choice where parents may send their children to any school in the district.

Montclair's citizens represent a wide range of socioeconomic, racial, and ethnic backgrounds. The public schools represent a microcosm of the world at large and offer an ideal setting to develop and demonstrate the viability and transferability of programs to larger segments of society.

Program Background

Along with its commitment to quality, integrated education, Montclair Public Schools have demonstrated a special commitment to technology. An atmosphere exists in the schools that welcomes technology and encourages purposeful exploration. Emphasizing the district's support, an elementary and a middle school science/technology magnet have been established to pioneer the use of technology in educational programs.

The district offers a number of technology-enriched programs in all schools and at all grade levels, from prekindergarten through high school. All Montclair students have opportunities to use technology in their educational activities. Available technologies in the district include television and video production, audiotapes, telecommunications, interactive video, video discs, computers, satellite communications, and robotics.

Program Mission

Montclair's primary purposes are to make effective use of technology to create stimulating learning environments for children and to promote overall school improvement.

Overview of the Program

While the Montclair Schools incorporate a wide variety of technologies in its programs, the most extensive use of technology in the district is in the area of computers. The number of district computers has increased from only 5 during the 1982 school year to 500 in the 1988 school year. Computers are becoming important mediums for both instruction and management. This section will provide an overview of the district's commitment to its educational technology program as well as its capacity to strengthen the program over time.

Planning for a Technological Future

Montclair's substantial investment in computer hardware, software, staff training, curriculum development, and personnel clearly reflects the district's recognition of the computer as a "one in several centuries" phenomenon. The district believes that appropriate computer use improves instruction and results in significant changes in the educational system. In addition to the commitment of its own funds, the district has aggressively sought and obtained additional funding and support from the United States Department of Education, the New Jersey State Department of Education, the New Jersey State Legislature, private foundations, and businesses.

Montclair's use of computers for educational purposes dates back to 1977, when computer-assisted instruction was introduced. Five years later, a town-wide Computer Advisory Committee was formed to help design the district's plan for the schools' computer program. With representation from school administrators, teachers, students, parents, and industry, the committee introduced a comprehensive plan to implement a prekindergarten through grade 12 computer training and instructional program. While that plan has been modified several times since its introduction, it provided an important beginning for the extended use of computers in the Montclair Schools.

The plan called for an extensive staff development and training program. The committee recognized the teacher as the critical variable in the effective use of computers. Adopting the committee's plan, the district initiated an intensive training program for 60 Montclair teachers and administrators. Bank

Street College provided training in computer literacy, LOGO computer language, and applying LOGO to specific curriculum areas.

The advisory committee also recommended the development of an elementary and a middle school science/technology magnet. Support for the establishment of these magnets clearly reflected a belief in the importance of technology in children's education.

Improving Education Through the Application of Technology

Major and rapid growth in district computer use began after the receipt of a federal grant. Five years ago, Montclair was one of only twelve districts in the nation to receive an "Improving Education Through the Application of Technology" grant from the United States Department of Education. Combining district and grant resources, Montclair developed a highly successful demonstration program for instructional technology.

The purpose of the federal grant was to produce and demonstrate a computer-based instructional program that would improve teaching methods, enhance teacher/student interactions, and strengthen student learning. The two science/technology magnet schools were designated as project sites.

The entire instructional staffs of these two magnet schools participated in extensive inservice training, again conducted by Bank Street College. The primary focus of the training was to help teachers develop ways to enhance students' problem-solving and thinking skills. Three 40-hour training workshops were offered during the first project year:

- "Using Word Processing to Enhance the Teaching of Writing,"
- "LOGO as a Medium for Teaching Problem-Solving and Thinking Skills," and
- "Using Microcomputers in Science Education."

Teacher questionnaires rated the workshops very highly. Principal observations noted that teachers enthusiastically incorporated the workshop ideas in their classes.

Weekly follow-up meetings with Bank Street staff supplemented the training. The trainers observed the teachers, provided feedback, and conducted monthly meetings. Teachers were encouraged to become peer trainers and coaches.

Curriculum development activities involving administrators, teachers, and parents followed the first project inservice and resulted in a comprehensive prekindergarten through grade 12 computer curriculum resource book and guide.

167

This document contains inservice training materials, strategies for teaching, sample lessons, student products, and networking materials.

During the second project year, additional staff were trained and further curriculum improvements were initiated. Eventually, over 300 Montclair staff members received computer training. All of the training occurred at the school building level so that teachers could enjoy and profit from collegial learning opportunities that enabled peer support systems to emerge. These were important factors in the district's successful incorporation of computers into instructional programs.

Another result of the federal project was the participation of Mount Hebron, the middle school science/technology magnet, in piloting the *Voyage of the Mimi* program. This instructional program uses the study of whales to provide a highly motivating starting point for a rich interdisciplinary study of science and mathematics topics. The *Mimi* combines video, computers, and print material in an exciting learning activity. The program was developed by Bank Street College under contract with the United States Department of Education. It is now available for distribution to all schools.

At the conclusion of the federal project, Montclair's elementary and middle schools had computer labs, technology-trained teachers, and technology curriculum and resource materials. The two science/technology magnets became demonstration sites for computer applications in education.

Montclair High School

Growth in the use of technology at the high school paralleled that of the other schools. Today, applications of technology can be found in all aspects of the high school community. Computers are used as instructional tools in classrooms ranging from science to special education to English. Seven computer labs are currently in operation and serve over 1,000 students.

Applied technology is particularly evident in the business education and industrial arts programs. Courses such as word processing, information processing, and computer publishing use state of the art equipment to teach business skills. Another high school course applies high technology to program robotic devices to perform mechanical tasks.

In the English department, computers help students hone their writing skills. Special education students take a course called "Thinking and Computers" that strengthens language skills. In science, computers are incorporated with laboratory work. This is most evident in physics, where simulations and data analyses are performed with a variety of software. In mathematics, computers help students strengthen their problem-solving skills.

168

Montclair High School participates in the Electronic Information Exchange System, a computer network operating statewide via modem to send messages and obtain information from other member schools and organizations.

Technology at Montclair High School is applied to management functions as well as curriculum areas. Attendance, grade reporting, scheduling, budgets, and student records have all been computerized. Few aspects of the instructional and administrative programs remain untouched by computers.

The Montclair Public School system's use of computer technology continues to evolve, moving from a literacy and programming focus to the full linkage of computers with the teaching/learning process. As experience and expertise with technology grow, new programs are introduced, piloted, and evaluated. Issues of equity and access are also comprehensively addressed.

Computers at the Elementary School

One very promising program has emerged at Watchung School, the system's elementary science/technology magnet. Supported by grants from the Florence and John Schumann Foundation, 3rd- and 4th-grade technology-enhanced classrooms were established. Each of these experimental classes were equipped with 12 Apple IIGS computers, 4 printers, a digital display projection screen, and a video disc player.

The availability of this technology and administrative support enabled teachers to restructure the teaching and learning process by managing instruction and information in a different way. No longer functioning as a channel through which most information flows, teachers began operating more as managers and coaches. Teachers and children were exploring together, searching data and employing critical thinking skills to make judgments. Working with the computers, students have greatly increased their interactions with each other. Excitement, sharing, and discovery take place at the computer in ways that never occur with pencil and paper.

Because technology has not been separated from learning, traditional subjects have been enhanced. For example, in science and mathematics, computers are helping to make abstract concepts more concrete. One project allows students to construct a robot using Lego building blocks and then program its movements using the LOGO language. Through this activity, students have hands-on learning in ratio, proportion, gears, friction, and a host of other topics. In language arts, word processing has improved students' writing by making editing much easier. Other language arts software also provide motivating simulation activities that improve writing skills. Databases are enriching social studies by helping students organize data into meaningful information.

Probably the most significant impact of computers on student learning in the experimental classes has been the development of problem-solving abilities. Students are trained to work in problem-solving teams to make informed decisions by analyzing a situation, plotting strategies, putting them into effect, and then checking solutions.

Another important benefit of the experimental classes is their positive effect on at-risk students. The ready availability of computer hardware and software permitted teachers to individualize instructional sequences for varying student learning levels. Furthermore, computers offered a multisensory approach to learning that was an alternative to the traditional instructional mode in which certain students were unable to succeed. Teachers noted that at-risk children especially seemed to enjoy learning with computers. As the children found opportunities to express themselves in creative ways and to interact noncompetitively with their peers on learning activities, their self-confidence grew.

> I like computers because I can have fun and learn at the same time. It helps me look at things in a different way. The computers make problem solving easier for me. I learn a lot more.
>
> - Watchung student

Computer-enhanced classrooms provide more equitable access to knowledge. Learning opportunities that would be available only to students who could afford to have computers in their own homes are now accessible to all children. Use of challenging software and opportunities to write their own software helped children integrate learning and apply critical thinking skills to their work.

After an evaluation of the program documented educational benefits to children in the experimental classes, the project was expanded to the entire school. Every class at Watchung School merges computers with the regular instructional program. The school, by fully incorporating technology, has become a building filled with active, rather than passive, learners in which children generate new learning for each other.

To ensure the continued success of the full integration of technology into the school's instructional program, the building principal maintains an ongoing teacher support and training program. A partnership with staff from Rutgers University provides workshops for Watchung teachers. Additionally, Watchung staff provide inservice activities for their peers in topics such as applications of new software or their own successful classroom teaching practices. Opportunities are offered for teachers to attend out-of-district technology conferences and then share their experiences with colleagues. Teachers are encouraged to observe each other and to collaborate on ways to merge technology with learning.

Townwide Advisory Committee

The townwide computer advisory committee, under the direction of a central office administrator, monitors the progress of computer use at the science/technology magnets and other district schools and disseminates successful practices. While the district leadership clearly endorses the full integration of technology into the educational program, the district also adopts the position that there is no one best way to use technology. Teacher experimentation and innovation is encouraged and supported. There is clear agreement that technology is an important medium of instruction, taking its place alongside print and other learning materials.

Program Evaluation

The scope of the district applications of technology requires continuous monitoring, evaluation, and revision. Evaluation techniques include:

- Standardized test results
- Student surveys
- Teacher critiques
- Classroom observations
- Staff and student interviews.

While student achievement on standardized tests cannot be attributed solely to the use of technology, evaluations indicate that planned technology use positively affects students' scores. Montclair has the highest student achievement record among New Jersey's urban districts.

Student surveys and interviews clearly and consistently indicate preferences for using computers for learning. Such evaluation methods also reveal student confidence and understanding of the applications of technology.

Teachers who regularly use technology in their classes express enthusiasm for its use as a way to improve their classroom practices. They note positive changes in students' learning, behavior, and attitudes.

> I now see myself as a learner sharing ideas with my students. Teaching has become more dynamic and challenging but certainly not

easier. It took me several months before I became comfortable with using technology in my instructional program. Now, I couldn't imagine teaching without it.

-Montclair teacher

Strongest Features of the Program

Montclair's plan for technology has been successful because the district leadership has instituted and maintained important components of that plan. These include:

- A comprehensive staff training and ongoing teacher support programs,
- Adequate technology that permitted increased staff and student access,
- A provision to ensure equity of use for all students,
- The development of technology applications based on research and successful classroom practices,
- Evaluation and revision of applied technology pilot programs,
- Linking technology and learning, and
- Identification of potential funding or technology donation sources.

Through careful and continuous planning, Montclair Public Schools are using technology to fully participate in the information age. While technology cannot solve the myriad educational problems schools face, Montclair's experience is that the appropriate integration of technology with instruction can lead to substantial improvements in the processes of teaching and learning.

Integrating Technology into the Elementary Curriculum

Contacts: Claire B. Passantino, Technology Specialist
William R. Thomas, Principal
210 E. Broad St.
Falls Church, VA 22046
(703) 241-7600

District Background

Falls Church City is a small suburban community in northern Virginia and a part of the greater Washington, D.C., area. The elementary school enrollment is approximately 550 students K-5 and is housed in two buildings. The community is extremely supportive of its schools, which is demonstrated through active parental participation and adequate funding. Student achievement as measured by standardized tests is consistently high, in spite of the fact that our student population is very diverse. School-based management has allowed us to be extremely responsive to student and curricular needs. The community and school encourage an openness and receptivity to new ideas, demonstrate a willingness to put forward considerable effort, and maintain high expectations for the students and the school program.

Program Mission

It has always been our intention that our computer use mirror our thinking and attitudes about how children learn and the way schools should function. During the last six years, we have tried to use computers and other forms of advanced technology in a variety of ways to help students learn, to improve the effectiveness of the instructional program, to improve the quality of the curriculum offered, and to help our school function more productively.

We look forward to the day when the computer has no more mystique than the filmstrip projector, when it becomes just one more device to enhance learning. It may be of interest that we use minimal CAI (computer-assisted instruction) or CMI (computer-managed instruction) in our school setting. Instead, we emphasize using computers to develop higher order thinking skills and processes; and because our student population is small and we know the students so well, we do not rely on computers to monitor instructional levels.

Program Overview

Each 1st grade classroom in the K-1 building has a computer with printer. First grade students use computers for mathematics instruction using LOGO and other math software. The computer is used to generate a weekly, first grade newspaper with increased direct computer input from students as the school year progresses. The special education teacher uses early childhood software with students who have problems with beginning learning tasks at the K-1 level.

In the 2-5 school, we have classroom computers, a full lab of 25 Commodore computers, and a mini-lab of 13 Apple computers. Many classroom computers have printers, and all lab computers are networked to printers. Two LCD (liquid crystal display) projection devices are available for use throughout the school. The diversity of hardware settings allows for a variety of instructional delivery formats.

All students use computers for one to three hours per week in various curricular areas. The number of computers and their locations are based on program goals. We have found that certain activities are best done in a lab setting, whereas the classroom is preferable for other activities.

Because of our confidence in the ability of our teachers to meet new challenges, we have given teachers ownership of the process of integrating the computer into the curriculum. Thus, teachers are responsible for planning and implementing computer lessons for their own classes.

How We Got Started

As is the case in many elementary schools, none of our elementary staff members possessed any computer knowledge prior to the start of computer integration. At that time, using a filmstrip projector was considered a high-tech event.

During the 1981-82 school year, we were selected to participate in the United States Department of Education "Interactive Video Disc Project." This project provided us with our first microcomputer. To illustrate just how naive we were: When we attempted to turn the computer on for the first time, we thought the machine was broken. No matter how hard we pressed the power indicator light, it refused to go on. Then we discovered the on/off switch. We realized that we had a great deal to learn!

Our first objective was to provide teachers with generous access to computers. Then we capitalized on their interest and initiative by holding inservice workshops and paying for graduate-level courses. Later, as more equipment was acquired and the tasks became more involved, a technology specialist was hired to assist with equipment, software evaluation and selection, and ongoing staff development. Further evaluation of our program determined that a computer aide was needed to handle the daily management of the computer labs.

Outstanding teachers, administrative encouragement, and technical support for teacher efforts have brought our program to its current level.

Where We Are Now

As improved programs and software become available, we continue to modify and replace portions of our current programs and activities.

We have used the computer language LOGO for more than six years. LOGO was selected because of its versatility and ability to address abstract thinking and problem-solving skills. For the last four years, LOGO instruction has been provided during one mathematics period per week for all grade 2-5 classes throughout most of the school year.

Initially, teachers taught LOGO to the students by encouraging them to make "discoveries." In subsequent years, this method resulted in a duplication of activities that students had done previously. We found a need to bring structure to the LOGO curriculum to assure that students could work on "discovering" different things at subsequent grade levels. This format has been successful for our program. First and second grade students learn about spatial relationships, shape recognition, patterns, and 90-degree turns. Third grade classes concentrate on acute and obtuse angles and triangles. Fourth graders work with polygons, circles, and ordered pairs. Students in fifth grade explore music by computer, binary codes (sprites), four-quadrant graphing, and projects with pattern blocks and their geometric properties.

Although LOGO continues to be a big part of our math curriculum, other effective mathematics software programs have been incorporated to match our curriculum needs. Some of these include *Bumble Games* and *Bumble Plot* for coordinate geometry; *Easy Graph* for generating graphs; a compendium of programs for computational skills drill and practice; and problem-solving software to practice memory-building, discrimination skills, and more advanced problem-solving strategies.

Besides LOGO, our early experiences with the computer included great successes using word processing with special education students. When taught word-processing skills, learning-disabled students who were reluctant writers began producing lengthy, well-written papers. These students began to express themselves effectively through writing—something they had rarely done before. We suspected that word processing could help all students with their writing and might easily fit into the instructional program.

Writing skills have long been emphasized with our students, and our Writing Skills Curriculum has been in place for more than 12 years. This program provides skill goals and expectations for students and teachers in creative and expository writing. Staff members have also participated in workshops and graduate courses, including a local Bay-Area Writing Project. Word processing is now an integral part of our writing program.

Currently, 2nd grade teachers introduce the computer as a word-processing tool during language arts class. Students are taught to find the keys on the keyboard and encouraged to use both hands. Simple word-processing activities are provided during the course of the year.

Third grade students begin to learn keyboarding using the software package *Microtype: The Wonderful World of Paws*. Classroom sets of "Typeright" keyboards are also used for keyboarding practice. Teachers assign writing projects to be completed on the computer. These assignments give students reasons and reinforcement for word processing and keyboarding. Keyboarding and word-processing activities begun at Grade 3 are extended at Grades 4 and 5.

Word processing has been used to produce student newspapers, to "publish" student writing as part of the writing process, and to compile an annual literary magazine of student work. One 5th grade class even used word processing to communicate with pen pals via modem.

Because of the limited instructional time available and the need for constant practice, keyboarding remains problematic. Word processing is an individualized activity that requires one computer per student and cannot be done without easy access to a printer. Rotating students through one classroom computer takes an inordinate amount of time. Therefore, most word-processing instruction is done in the full computer lab or mini-lab where computers are networked to printers. Using parent volunteers has given us even more flexibility with word processing because some teachers prefer to work in their rooms and send students to the lab when ready. Word processing is an effective addition to the instructional program but is not without its time, organizational, and financial constraints.

Using technology to enhance the science, social studies, and health programs is a challenge because of the difficulty of identifying quality materials that match our curriculum objectives. One of our current favorites, *Oregon Trail*, is a good simulation to illustrate the struggles the pioneers experienced. This correlates well with the "Family of Man" Grade 3 social studies unit on the California Gold Rush. The *Where in the U.S.A. Is Carmen Sandiego?* program provides students with an opportunity to extend and reinforce information learned in the 4th grade social studies program and practice library skills. At Grades 4 and 5, we have integrated *The Voyage of the **Mimi*** into the science curriculum. Not only does this program use videotapes and computer software, but it also includes laboratory probes that are attached to the computer and used as measuring tools in hands-on scientific experiments. Student appreciation of science has increased to such an extent that we plan to use *Second Voyage of the **Mimi*** at the 5th grade level.

Technology is used in numerous settings outside the regular classroom. A wide variety of reading and language arts software is used in the ESL classes and by the Chapter I reading teacher. Besides using the computers for instructional purposes, the special education teachers have found test-scoring software and programs to help produce well-constructed IEPs (individual educational plans). Even the physical education teachers use computers to record student physical fitness statistics. Our library is in the process of moving towards a computerized circulation and cataloging system. And computers are used by after-school clubs such as the Technology Club and the Young Astronauts.

Program Evaluation

It has been difficult to evaluate the impact of new technologies, especially the computer, on student achievement. We have observed increases in students' writings and abilities to solve increasingly abstract problems. However, neither improvement can be attributed solely to computer use, since our total instructional program is never static. We are continually finding new and better ways to teach language arts and mathematics, thus making it difficult to isolate and evaluate the different components in our educational "mix."

We can point to a few instances that indicate that computer use has made a cognitive difference. For example, several years ago we replaced one mathematics period per week with a LOGO class at Grades 2 through 5. We had no way of knowing how this change would affect our students' standardized test results. Interestingly, the scores were as high as before, and they have been as high or higher each year since. Although test scores are a positive indicator, of more importance to us is our day-to-day observation of students enthusiastically and productively engaged in learning.

Strongest Feature of the Program

The strongest feature of our use of technology is a persistent effort to integrate the computer into all aspects of the school curriculums. Additionally, realistic support has been provided to teachers to use technology effectively. Our technical support has increased from virtually none to our current staff of a professional technology specialist to work with teachers, hardware, software, and curriculum, and a teacher's aide to assist in the computer labs on a daily basis.

The ability to respond quickly to the needs of students and curriculum is another strength. This includes a keen awareness of student needs and technological advances, creative management, and a willingness to reallocate available funds.

Finally, our program reflects a vision of the possible. We make every effort to perceive technological advances as opportunities and challenges.

Future of the Program

Because of the positive orientation of the staff and community toward technology and its important role in education, we anticipate continued change, growth, and improvement in our use of existing and emerging technologies. Much of what we have been doing will probably continue with modifications as we learn of new and better techniques and approaches.

As we learn more about the effective application of technology to learning, we will undoubtedly place greater emphasis on meeting individual student needs through technology. Since the ability to access information is of increasingly critical importance in our society, we are beginning to teach database search skills and use databases in the content subjects. Interactive video disc technology will be used more and more within the next few years. Finally, with the advent of telecommunications and interactive satellite television, distance learning will significantly increase the range of learning opportunities for students, staff, and community.

* * *

It is important to remember that change happens in small steps. The challenge now is to take enough small steps to keep up with the giant steps that technology is making in our world every day. No wonder that many educators are fearful of technology. It is quite possible that we are seeing the beginning of activities that will dramatically alter schooling as we have known it. But, in spite of the fact that technology's ever-changing nature is a constant frustration, its promises for the future are a visionary's delight.

Integrating Technology into Curriculum

Contact: Steve Williams
              Forest Hills Central High School
              5901 Hall Street
              Grand Rapids, MI 49506

Program Background

In 1984, Forest Hills Central High School, a suburban high school of 1,000 students in grades 9-12 located near Grand Rapids, Michigan, began to look at the future of its educational program. A group of business leaders, parents, college educators, administrators, teachers, and students was formed to make recommendations about the overall directions the district should focus on. They produced a study titled *Focus on the Decade Ahead*.

After one year of visitations, data gathering, and issues analysis, it became apparent that certain educational changes needed to take place if our students are to be successful in the world of the 21st century. One of the study's strongest recommendations was for the district to focus on effective use of the technologies that were already significantly affecting the business world and transforming our society from an industrial-based economy to one driven by information. The world was changing, but our educational program remained one designed to meet the needs of a society that was rapidly disappearing.

A study on the need to construct a new high school occurred simultaneously with the educational program. It became apparent that as old educational programs could not support new educational needs, buildings designed to support educational programs of the past would not be adequate to meet the needs of an information-age curriculum. We knew that access to information from a variety of resources located in various places in this country and abroad is essential to support an educational program that focuses on developing thinking and information processing skills—the key skills needed to be successful in the 21st century. The question then arose, "How do you provide a facility that enables students, teachers, administrators, and staff access to the information they may need today and in the future?"

The answer—network the facility.

Selecting a Communications System

After a significant amount of searching on our part, and with the assistance of a consultant from Wayne State University, we discovered a communications system that would network all instructional and administrative areas of the school for video, voice, and data communications. The system—TEKNET—is divided into administrative and instructional components coordinated through video, computer, and telephone switching systems.

The instructional component, which is housed in the media center, consists of a bank of videotape recorders and access to the local cable system and two satellite receivers. Access to resources through these technologies is handled through a control panel and television monitor in each classroom and office. The control panel consists of a television channel selector, a telephone (used to access the VCRs and act as a remote control for them, as well as being a regular telephone), two data lines allowing classroom access to databases, and two RF (radio frequency) connectors allowing internal audio/video broadcasts between any combination of rooms and/or offices in the building.

The administrative area houses the administrative part of the system, which controls the class change time, public address system, the time appearing on a dedicated channel on all TV monitors, a vandal alarm system, and an electronic bulletin board for announcements.

Program Implementation

While the nuts and bolts of this communications system are intriguing, the system is of little significance if it is not used. The key to achieving maximum use was, and continues to be, a heavy emphasis on staff development consisting of three components. First, each staff member received an individualized session on basic operation and uses of the system. Second, and more important, a long-term plan giving each curriculum department a one-day inservice during school time was developed and focused on the following elements:

- Research on effective uses of technology in learning,
- Overview of technologies and their capabilities,
- Brainstorming potential uses of technologies,
- Effective learning and teaching activities and methods,
- Classroom use and management alternatives,
- Identification and evaluation of resources, and
- Technical and other support available.

The final element consists of coaching and support from the computer/video video paraprofessionals and myself. This means taking the teachers' ideas and translating them into specific instructional activities that can be first piloted and then used in general classroom applications. We have found that without this last phase of staff development, little real change in instructional design and delivery would have taken place.

Current Uses

World Studies. World studies classes, a required course for seniors, focuses on understanding concepts that interconnect the countries of the world. Through the use of technologies, our students have the opportunity to gather and analyze information from sources around the world that previously have been available only to news media and government. For example, by viewing news programs from Lebanon, via satellite, our students see first-hand the effects of the violence in that conflict-torn nation. Seeing news broadcasts from different countries with different perspectives on the same issues gives our students the opportunity to develop analytical skills based on real-world experiences.

World studies students have direct classroom access through a computer and modem to GEMNET's Global Information Network, a group of databases providing news stories from developing countries, United Nations speeches and resolutions, and an electronic mail system to and from students in other countries. This type of hard-to-find information is a key element in achieving our goal: helping students develop the ability to analyze complicated concepts and issues from different perspectives.

In addition, students in these classes are required to prepare a video or multimedia presentation demonstrating their research skills and analytical skills, understanding of world issues and concepts, and ability to communicate through a script and visual presentation. In the near future, we will be using Hypercard to develop these presentations by letting the students integrate video, graphics, and text. The TEKNET communications system will allow these presentations to be stored in a central databank and shared with other classes.

In evaluating the use of these technologies and more important this approach to learning, we have found a significant decrease in the number of students who have failed this course since this approach was developed (some semesters the failure rate is zero). During parent-teacher conferences, numerous parents mention that their children regularly discuss world issues and events with them. The media presentations, in general, are outstanding for summarizing major concepts and issues, and a number of students each semester ask that a videotape be made of their presentations so that they can show it to their parents or grandparents. In addition, preliminary results of studies involving students who prepare a presentation that visually portrays their understanding of issues and concepts shows that they have at least an 80 percent retention rate six months after the end of the course compared to a 20 percent retention rate for students in a traditionally taught class.

Earth Science. A computer and modem through the TEKNET system is also used by earth science students to access weather data from the NOAA database. With this raw data, students plot weather maps, learn about the movement of weather fronts, analyze and predict local weather forecasts, and, above all, get real-world experiences in an area of science that will affect them all their lives.

Initial evaluation of this unit indicates that students develop a deeper understanding of weather concepts as evidenced by improved test scores and the ability to predict weather using the same methodology as professional meteorologists.

Art. Computer technology is being used at Forest Hills Central in all art classes. Students use graphics software for a myriad projects requiring them to use their creative talents. For example, students attach a video camera to a computer to capture an image that they then manipulate with the computer software to create a new image. The technologies have become nearly as essential as the paintbrush. In fact, they have opened the wonderful world of art to a whole new group of students who have been interested in computers but not art. At the same time, art students who feared computers now develop individual computer art shows.

At regular intervals, the computer art shows are broadcast through the TEKNET system to all classes. So as the students showcase their talents, the art department has a built-in advertising campaign for their classes.

Television Journalism Course. The TEKNET communications system has given birth to a new course—television journalism. The course focuses on a weekly school news program—FORECAST EXPOSURE—developed entirely by the students. Students rotate through tasks that involve scriptwriting, camera and audio work, directing, and producing. The program generally revolves around a Phil Donahue format in which students can respond to a panel discussion directly in their classroom via telephone. The subject matter has included drugs on campus, teen suicide, graduation requirements, college admissions, the role of the student council, the "best" places to go for spring vacation, and question-and-answer sessions with the superintendent and principal. The course and programs have been an unqualified success in developing communications skills for the students involved and providing a communications forum for students, teachers, and administrators.

Writing and Technology. The National School Board Association and Cable News Network (CNN) combined forces to offer a unique service called News

Access that utilizes CNN's weekly news summary as a vehicle for numerous learning opportunities. News access provides a complete learning guide, summary sheet, and ideas for classroom activities in all areas of the curriculum through COMPUSERVE, a national telecommunications service we access through the data lines in the TEKNET system.

Although activities abound for many learning purposes, we focus on using these sources as a vehicle for creative writing activities in language arts, social studies, and science classes. In as many classes as possible, students use word processing for prewriting, writing, and revising their creative writing assignments.

Since we began using News access, we have found students' writing to be of higher quality in terms of development of ideas, grammar, and punctuation. Students' concentration levels have also increased.

Business and Telecommunications. The business department uses the TEKNET communications system wiring to set up an electronic bulletin board and electronic mail between two of our computer labs. This allows our students hands-on experience with telecommunications without the expense and complications of accessing an external system.

Math and Technology. In 1985, a teacher of consumer and general math became frustrated with the results from those classes. The students (11th and 12th graders) could not apply the math skills they were being taught. They knew 40 percent of 5 was 2 but could not figure the mortgage rate on a house.

To overcome this, several changes were made. First, the textbook became a supplemental resource to a series of real-world learning activities that incorporated the math skills. For example, students selected a career they were interested in, researched the take-home pay they would earn, went to a car dealer to get the price of a car, went to at least two places for a car loan, and then figured out the amount they could afford to pay for a car based upon the price of the car, the loan payment, and their income. These activities take up three of the five days a week, with basic math skill development worked on the other two days.

Basic skills development is done with two technology-based resources. Two days a week, half of the class works on a computer-managed math skill program from S.R.A. Students perform a pretest placing them in a sequential series of lessons in which they must pass each lesson with at least an 80 percent accuracy rate before proceeding to the next lesson. These records are stored on the computer for review by the teacher. The other half of the class works with their teacher and a videodisc package from Systems Impact. The videodisc contains direct skills instruction (taught using methods addressing different learning styles), provides guided practice, and gives tests for each skill. The teacher monitors the activity of each student, answers questions, and advances the videodisc to the next skill level when all of the students have passed the test for that skill.

The results of this approach have been overwhelming. In two and a half years, no student has received lower than a C in this course, impressive considering many of these students had failed math classes before and the tests given are twice as difficult as those given to students in the previous classes using traditional methods. In addition, three weeks of additional skills are taught in this class because students learn the skills much more quickly than in the previous approach to the class. Another major benefit has been the marked decrease in discipline problems (students in this class tended to have discipline problems in other classes).

Teaching and Learning Implications

After three years of refocusing our high school with the assistance of the TEKNET communications system and a variety of other technologies and instructional resources, we are finding the learning environment has become more learner-centered and less teacher-directed. The teacher manages the environment and acts as a "learning coach" and instructional designer. The teacher designs learning activities that develop a variety of thinking and learning skills that the learner uses to transform information into knowledge. The important implication is that while in the future new information may make previously-learned knowledge obsolete, the students have mastered the skills needed to transform this new information into new knowledge. Technological tools allow this educational transformation to take place.

Obstacles

With any change, especially changes of this magnitude, there is resistance. Teachers who have taught with the same style for 20 to 30 years and students who are used to traditional methods of education were initially hesitant. However, the active nature of these new teaching and learning methods, along with the participatory nature of inservices, has largely overcome resistance.

Another obstacle was financing the technologies and related resources. Fortunately, our community voted funding to build the new school with the TEKNET communications system, and the district administration budgeted the needed dollars for staff development. And because much of the educational change was based upon the use of multiple resources instead of textbooks, a portion of the finances for resources came from monies that would have gone for textbooks.

184

The remaining obstacle is the development of additional methods of evaluating learning. The questions are "How do you evaluate thinking and related skills?" and "How do you evaluate the impact of technologies?" To answer these questions we have contracted with Wayne State University to develop evaluation models for assessing learning outcomes and the effectiveness of using technologies in the learning process.

*   *   *

While much of what I have written about involves inanimate objects of technology, these alone could not have accomplished the results I have noted— nor could they provide the expected results in the future without education centered around the ancient proverb,

Tell me, I forget.

Show me, I remember.

Involve me, I understand.

And this will not happen without the most critical element of all— PEOPLE—especially dedicated, knowledgeable teachers, administrators, and community members. Fortunately, our district is blessed with an abundance of these people who deserve the credit for present and future accomplishments.

Corona-Norco Unified School District:
Exemplary Programs Integrating Technology

Contact: Thomas Wilson
Coordinator of Technological Education
Corona-Norco Unified School District
Corona, California

The Corona-Norco Unified School District, serving both communities in California, is a suburban district located about forty miles east of Los Angeles. The district has a K-12 enrollment in its 26 schools of 20,000 students, of which 31 percent are Hispanic.

Overview of the Program

The Corona-Norco Unified School District has engaged in short-term and long-range planning to effectively integrate technology into all curricular areas and grade levels to revitalize and transform instruction—to change the ways teachers teach and students learn. To finance the acquisition of equipment, the district looked for help from a number of sources. Parent groups bought or donated thousands of dollars worth of hardware and software. Major companies such as AT&T, Ford, General Dynamics, and others loaned or donated equipment or helped the district buy it. Local businesses contributed, too. Grants from the California State Department of Education also gave the district a financial boost.

The following is a brief description of four of the district's exemplary programs that successfully integrate technology into the curriculum. Two of the practices, the first and last, can be used at all grade levels. The second program is a secondary course, and the third program is an elementary intervention.

Video Microscopy

The Corona-Norco Unified School District is very pleased with the success it has experienced with the Video Microscopy Teaching Station in elementary and secondary schools. The teaching station can be ordered in several different configurations; however, the system used most in the district is from Video Systems, Inc., a subsidiary of Southland Instruments. This system incorporates the use of a color video camera on a boom, large-screen monitor, small control monitor, stereoscopic dissecting microscope, binocular-compound microscope, electronic pointer, dual goose-neck fiber optic variable-intensity lights, and a mobile cart with a security cover. The system is expandable and can be connected to a video cassette recorder-player to produce lessons uniquely adapted to any program.

The video microscopy system is versatile, is easy to use, and serves several important purposes. The program is designed to improve student learning, stimulate cognitive development, create interest in science and science-related careers, provide effective large-group instruction, and allow the teacher to choose material that fits into the class structure and curriculum rather than being restricted to textual or prerecorded material.

Teachers and students can use the video camera to develop a lesson by selecting live specimens, photographs, or other printed materials to show to an entire class. Many lessons can be developed from just one slide.

When students view the television monitor, it may show a flower, for example, that has been placed on the copy stand. By changing the camera lens, the flower can be moved to the dissecting microscope. The flower can now be seen in more detail. The stamen and pistil are magnified. When the camera is moved to the stereo microscope, pollen grains become visible to the naked eye. And this entire exercise could have been recorded on videotape including the teacher's narrative.

The video microscopy system, using the stereoscopic dissection scope, can be used to show small organisms such as mites, fleas, spiders, soil, pollen, and plankton. It can also magnify parts of larger organisms up to 45 times. Students often bring their own specimens to school to view, record, and share with others. Students can even take their work home on videotape to share with their families.

The compound microscope is an essential part of the video microscopy system. It allows students to investigate the microbial world. Bacteria, protozoa, fungi, and microscopic nonliving samples can be magnified up to 1,000 times using this type of microscope. When asked to find water samples containing a variety of microbes, students can use this system to share their samples with the class. Specimens of special interest can also be recorded and played back for study at a later date.

The use of the Video Microscopy Teaching Station has become an important part of the science classroom environment. Students have learned to prepare slides and operate the equipment. They have observed such things as single-celled organisms, circulation within a living animal, insects and their structure, and plant and animal cells. This new technological tool makes students at both the elementary and secondary level more enthusiastic about science.

Design-Manufacturing Technology

The Design-Manufacturing Technology program at Corona Senior High School is an advanced industrial arts course for 12th grade students that combines lessons in drafting and metals. The two-semester course is designed to reinforce academic learning, promote creativity, role play industrial settings, and develop vocational skills. The program was funded primarily with vocational education monies.

Through the Design-Manufacturing program, students learn components of design, drafting, computer numerically controlled programming and machining, computer-aided drafting, and technical report writing. Students are also given the opportunity to study robotics, hydraulics, pneumatics, mechanics, and plastic injection molding. Each student's goal is to design and manufacture a high-quality, marketable product in a simulated industrial setting using state-of-the-art technological equipment.

During the first semester, students prepare for the task by using manual drawing and machining techniques. Assignments in basic print reading introduce the student to various numeric systems of measurement used in working drawings. These assignments explore common drawing standards, dimensioning, and shop notes used in manufacturing. Pictorial drawings are also covered to assist the student with visualizing the product.

During the second semester, emphasis is placed on computer systems, software, and product development. Before students begin computer-aided drafting, they review basic mechanical drawing concepts. The students learn to properly use tools on the drafting table while reviewing lettering, sketching, and production drawing techniques.

Once the students master the basics, computer-aided drafting is introduced. With the use of an IBM-compatible computer and Auto Cad software by Autodesk, Inc., students draw, edit, and plot working or pictorial drawings on the computer.

Once students have a basic understanding of print reading, mechanical drawing, and computer-aided drafting, they are introduced to the machine tool process. The first step in machine tooling involves learning to measure with rules and precision instruments such as micrometers, vernier calipers, and dial indicators. Students also perform exercises designed to develop an understanding of the standard engine lathe and milling machine.

With a strong emphasis placed on safety, computer-aided manufacturing is introduced as the final simulated industrial element. First, students work with computer numerically controlled (CNC) programming. Basic machine language "G" codes are reviewed for cutting actions on the CNC lathe and mill.

Each student writes a tool path program using the cartesian coordinate system. With the help of an initial working drawing, the students produce preliminary program sketches, which are drawn five times their actual size. The programs are then input into an Apple computer using the Emco-Maier "Link-up Box" software program. This software and computer system allows students to simulate machine turning, plot out tool path graphs, and print out data. The students are then ready to transmit the program to the host computer on the CNC lathe or mill. The finished products become reward for jobs well done.

Throughout the entire manufacturing process, students compile a technical report manual that applies and reinforces the academic learning. Word processing is incorporated. Each report includes a student-produced narrative description of the project, completed technical drawings, computer programs, tool path plots, and a quality control study.

Students' enthusiasm and interest run high when they are given the opportunity to design, draft, program, and manufacture products using technological machining systems. After successful completion of this class, students are better prepared for college-level engineering courses and entry into hi-tech industries.

Computer Checkout Program

The innovative, elementary school Computer Checkout Program provides students with assistance in using the computer. Students are trained in the use of microcomputer hardware and software in school. Parents of students in grades 4 to 6 are then permitted to "checkout" and take home the computer equipment and programs. At home, parents connect the computers to their own television sets and use the equipment to teach and reinforce the skills their children are learning in math and language arts. Radio Shack Color Computers, color television sets, and software programs are used in the program.

The Computer Checkout Program is intended to serve several purposes. The primary program objectives are to reinforce the basic skills through the use of computer-assisted instruction (CAI); increase interactive rather than passive use of leisure time; stimulate learning and cognitive development; increase instructional time; improve the learning environment at home; increase communication between teacher, parent, and child; and promote computer literacy.

The equipment and software are located in a classroom for CAI during the regular school day. The equipment and software are also available for parents of intermediate students to checkout during the week, and over holidays, weekends, and vacations during the school year. However, parents must first attend one of two orientation meetings offered during the year and complete a

Program Participant's Card. The training time required for both teachers and parents is minimal.

During a school's orientation meeting, the teacher explains to the parents the procedures used to check out and check in computers and software; gives instructions on the setup and use of equipment and software; and provides helpful hints concerning equipment security in the home, supervision of home use, and care and maintenance of the equipment. The classroom teachers pre-assign specific software programs to each family, taking into consideration students' needs. Parents may checkout two software packages and a computer for the same period of time.

The computer provides a well-designed teaching outline based on sound education principles. This is especially helpful for parents who are eager to help their children but have little or no teaching experience. The computer provides parents and children with the opportunity to learn together.

The Video Termpaper on Historical Subjects

The video termpaper is one of the most exciting new applications of research technology in school-site, library resource centers. The concept of a video termpaper involves the integration of various technologies, including videodisc, videotape, CD-ROM, on-line database retrieval services, and camcorders. Teams of students in both elementary and secondary schools in the Corona-Norco Unified School District have developed multimedia reports. The reports have been primarily on historical subjects.

Once a small group of three or four students has received its assignment from a teacher and selected a historical research topic, the team creates a pre-liminary outline for its report and conducts initial research. The students research the topic using the various sources of information in the school's library resource center. They begin by taking notes while looking through vari-ous books, periodicals, journals, and other print resources. Students find it valuable to review resource materials and select still and motion film clips from various videodiscs such as the Video Encyclopedia of the 20th Century.

The video encyclopedia is a set of 40 archival videodiscs from CEL Educa-tional Resources, which includes original stills and motion pictures of nearly every major event that has affected American culture since 1893. Students can also conduct additional research by going on line with a database retrieval ser-vice such as DIALOG, or employing Grolier's Electronic Encyclopedia, a CD-ROM application. DIALOG is a comprehensive information resource—a computer-based, on-line system allowing students instant access to summaries of articles and reports, detailed financial data, and directory listings of companies, statistics, and full-text articles and newswires from hundreds of databases. The service requires a computer, printer, modem, communications software, telephone connection, and subscription to DIALOG.

After the initial research is done, students begin writing their report's preliminary script. The team members meet to discuss their research and cooperatively develop the presentation's video production script, which incorporates printed resources, electronic database retrieval service information, still pictures, motion pictures from videodiscs, filming, and editing. The students meet several times to revise and improve the script and discuss the sets and techniques needed for filming and editing the production.

After several video rehearsals, the student team advances to the next phase, video production. Video production involves using video technology and equipment such as VCRs, video disc players, and camcorders as the tools of creation to develop an idea and explore a subject by sequencing visual images. The members of the team also film each other presenting portions of the narrative.

Once the filming is completed, post-production begins. Post-production consists of logging, editing, sound mixing, and narration. The logging and editing functions are done by the students on a control panel, player, and player-recorder. Sound production is done by interfacing stereo components and a microphone through a sound mixer.

The development of video termpapers enables students to cover selected topics more deeply and emerge from the video experience with greater retention than is gained from a traditional textbook approach. Students also expand their creative potential and develop technical knowledge and skills. Video production alone requires students to apply or develop new skills in mathematics, language arts, problem solving, drama, and research.

Video images can convey the subtleties of people, places, and events, and the feelings that events inspired. A textbook can tell a student—but not show a student. Video termpapers show students at their best.

Technology in Tippecanoe

Contact: Joanne Troutner
Coordinator for Instructional Support
Tippecanoe School Corporation
21 Elston Road
Lafayette, Ind.
(317) 474-2481

District Background

Tippecanoe School Corporation (TSC), Lafayette, Indiana, is in an area that is both rural and suburban. The school district forms a doughnut around the urban districts of Lafayette and West Lafayette. The northern end of the district holds suburban areas adjacent to Purdue University; the southern section possesses some of the richest farmland in the Midwest. This mixture provides an intermingling of approximately 7,500 students who attend the two 9-12 high schools, five 6-8 middle schools, and seven K-5 elementary schools. The technology program in Tippecanoe permeates each of these schools to varying degrees.

Program Background

The program resulted from a question asked by the TSC school board president about six years ago. The question was simple: "How do we know our students are learning what we say we are teaching?" The answer proved to be quite complex. Standardized test scores did not address the question for every section of the TSC curriculum. Report card grades were a general measure, but did not provide a true picture of what concepts students had mastered. TSC's inability to answer this question led to the development of a six- to eight-year plan for the implementation of a criterion-reference-based testing system throughout the corporation. The development and initial phases of this testing system pointed out the need for a technology system that would help with the individualized instructional needs identified by the tests.

This program currently affects the entire student population. The entire TSC technology program, as well as the curriculum portion (the Instructional Support System), was developed to provide teachers with the means to better identify individual students' learning needs. The purpose of these programs is seven fold:

1. To evaluate how well students are achieving the corporation's educational objectives.

2. To more clearly define academic strengths and weaknesses of individual students, as well as the entire student population.

3. To more clearly define instructional strengths and weaknesses.

4. To provide clearer direction for student remediation and advanced placement.

5. To improve the guidance and counseling of individual students based upon the student's specific skill level.

6. To allow staff, students, and parents to better focus on specific student needs, thus improving communication between interested parties.

7. To provide specific feedback for evaluating the appropriateness of curriculum objectives, particularly at the elementary school level.

The school district began working toward these goals by developing an administrative computer network. The IBM System 36 at the Central Office holds the curriculum objective database and the student information database for the entire district. System 36 computers at each of the high schools and middle schools are used for student information, attendance, and grade data.

To address the instructional implications of these goals, in October 1987, TSC purchased ten networked computer labs of at least 30 IBM PS/2 Model 25 workstations with a PS/2 Model 60 file server with 140 megabytes of hard disk storage. In addition, at the elementary level, a full complement of IBM basic skills software in the areas of reading, language arts, math, and keyboarding, and two word processing programs, a database management program, and LogoWriter were acquired. At the high schools, software bought included Microsoft Works and IBM basic skill programs in the areas of reading, language arts, math, keyboarding, science, and upper-level math programs. Software for the middle school labs included Microsoft Works, Linkway (an IBM hypertext tool), and basic skills programs.

The computer labs have been put into each elementary and high school with a minimum of building renovation, usually only the running of networking cables and rewiring to have adequate electricity. In two elementary schools that did not have room for a separate computer lab, the workstations are still networked, but two or three workstations are put into each room. The high school labs were put into the existing library media centers. Initial teacher training was conducted by IBM over teacher inservice days in October 1987. This involved becoming familiar with setting up access to courseware for students and being exposed to the courseware itself. IBM also provided onsite trainers for the first week of November who were available on a rotating basis in each building.

In December 1987, TSC created the position of Coordinator for Instructional Support. The Coordinator's duties include staff development and troubleshooting. As part of staff development, teachers were provided with support using the basic skills software at the elementary schools. The use of word processing was given the highest priority at the high schools. I provided a two-day unit on learning to use the word processor for the classes of any high school English teacher who wished to use the network. The key to our initial success was not only staff support, but the fact that staff members were not mandated to use the computer labs. The administration took the stance that the corporation was simply providing another tool for teachers to use with instruction.

Summer brought an intensive round of inservice workshops. Teachers in TSC had the option of taking sessions on Microsoft Works; a graphics program, Storyboard Plus; LogoWriter; curriculum integration for primary grades (K-3); and curriculum integration for intermediate grades (4-5). These workshops were conducted by the Coordinator for Instructional Support and a team of teachers who have developed expertise in these areas throughout the time the networks had been in operation.

Technology Projects

Summer also brought the addition of three special technology projects to TSC. First was the use of a student management system called Integrated Instructional Management Tool (IIMT). This program is currently being used on a pilot basis with the help of IBM. IIMT allows the teachers to have access to the TSC curriculum objective database stored on the Central Office System 36. The program allows teachers to make use of an electronic gradebook and track students' progress as related to each curriculum objective in the areas of language arts, math, science, and social studies. A test scanning program allows for machine scoring of multiple choice tests and sends these grades to the computer gradebook. Mastery on objectives can be updated on the basis of a grade from the gradebook or teacher observation. The system also allows for the development of an individualized prescription including library materials, textbook resources, and learning kits for the student who has not mastered an objective. In addition, IIMT will also set the starting place or "bookmark" in the basic skills for each student based on the stored mastery information.

A state-funded grant for a high school "Classroom Without Walls" brought about the second project. This endeavor provided students in three sections of Chemistry I with access to eight computers connected to the existing computer network in the school. Students and teachers use a variety of software developed by COMPress, Inc., Project Seraphim, Microsoft Works, and the IBM Math Exploration Toolkit. The teachers also have a liquid crystal display available for use with the teacher workstation. This allows teachers to show class statistics on a unit test from the computerized gradebook, to illustrate a graphing technique for use in a lab report, and to use the computer as an overhead with some of the software.

Students in the computer-using chemistry classes were offered instruction in using Microsoft Works during two afternoon sessions the week before school started. The teachers spent the summer designing lab reports that make use of the tools available in Microsoft Works. One example of computer integration is an experiment dealing with the thickness of an aluminum sheet. Students are introduced to the concept of accuracy and experimental precision as they use a spreadsheet to help view how their individual experimental data differ from an experimental average value. The template for the experiment is stored on the network for use by all students. The students use the graphing functions available in Microsoft Works to complete the lab report. Finally, the students send lab reports to Purdue University chemistry graduate students via modem for review before the reports are turned in to their teachers.

The third project, the Computer-in-the-Home or Buddy project was sponsored by private corporations with help from the Indiana Department of Education. Through this project, fourth-grade students at one elementary school have a ten-station, networked computer lab in each of their classrooms. These students also have a computer at their home. The students and their families were provided with an IBM PS/2 Model 25 with a 20 megabyte hard drive, a printer, a modem, and all the IBM basic skills programs, the entire Assistant series as tool software, a graphics program, and access to the Prodigy on-line information service. The teachers also have a machine in their homes.

Students have learned to use the word processor, graphics program, database manager, and the on-line information service. Homework assignments in these classes have included working on the keyboarding program, writing a story about the Pilgrims with parents' help, and using the weekly version of *Where Is Carmen Sandiego* from the information service. Database assignments on famous Indiana people have been developed. A database of information on the Purdue University basketball team has been used for writing assignments, learning to use the graphing program, and discovering the uses of a spreadsheet.

Program Funding and Staffing

TSC has chosen to fund the implementation of the Instructional Support System through building funds. The TSC has viewed this venture into technology as building a new school facility. In addition, the purchases have been spread over a three-year period. The only staff position added as a result of this move into the world of technology has been that of Coordinator for Instructional Support.

The technology requires no building-level manager. Special workshops have been held, however, for the library media specialists from each building. These professionals have assumed the role of technology expert in the building. Initial training was conducted over teacher inservice days. Additional training opportunities on Microsoft Works, Writing Assistant, Filing Assistant, Storyboard Plus, and curriculum integration were held on one of the teacher inservice days in October 1988. Training on Excelsior Grade, the computerized gradebook available throughout the system, was held during Christmas vacation. Further workshops are planned for future summers.

The philosophy behind the staff development has been to help a number of teachers become experts on various programs. Decentralization of technology knowledge has been the guiding premise of all training plans. This decentralization is furthered by the use of a Council for Instructional Support, chaired by the Coordinator. This group of technology experts, at least one from each building, meets once a month. Meetings include time to discuss what is working well in each building and what areas need attention. Time is also devoted to a training segment. The training has ranged from integrating LogoWriter into the 2nd grade math problem-solving curriculum to the use of a liquid crystal display to the use of the Prodigy on-line information service.

The instructional support system operates under the guidance of the Administrative Assistant for Program Development and the Assistant Superintendent for Instruction. These individuals are responsible for the corporation-level systems involved with the administrative applications of technology and oversee the position of Coordinator for Instructional Support. Supervision of the day-to-day operation and maintenance of the instructional computer networks, development of technology training programs, selection of appropriate software, and development of curriculum integration strategies is the responsibility of the Coordinator for Instructional Support.

Program Evaluation

Because this program has been in place for less than two years, evaluation is just beginning. The first stage was a survey conducted in mid-October on how computer time was being used at each elementary school. The results were presented to the school board in February 1989. The survey shows that the majority of teachers in TSC are currently using computer time with drill-and-practice software with heavy emphasis on spelling. Use of language arts software dominates over the basic skills software available for math. The integration of word processing into the elementary curriculum is sporadic.

The results of this survey help the Coordinator for Instructional Support see the areas where more curriculum integration, and subsequently staff development, is needed. Survey results from April 1989 will be used to see what differences, if any, were seen later in the school year.

Strongest Feature of the Program

The strongest feature of this program has been the commitment to staff development. Too often school districts buy state-of-the-art equipment but fail to spend the time and money necessary for staff training and development. The TSC has not made this mistake. The district has added the position of Coordinator for Instructional Support to oversee the ongoing staff development in the area of technology. The process of developing building experts and a cadre of people knowledgeable about a particular program has been highly successful. Any school district embarking on such a venture would be wise to consider the TSC model for staff development.

The future of technology in the Tippecanoe School Corporation is bright, with 1 computer for every 10 students. Plans are underway to work with database programs in the social studies curriculum, and use of the Prodigy on-line information service will be expanded in the future. The area of hypermedia will be explored. The implementation of a computerized library management system also looms in the future for TSC. Teachers will increasingly be able to pinpoint what concepts a particular student needs to master and to communicate this information more precisely to the parents. The concentration on using the computer as a tool will provide our students with a foundation that will serve them well as they enter the world and become productive citizens.

About the Authors

Barbara Bowman, Director of Graduate Studies, Erikson Institute, Chicago, Illinois.

Donna Jean Carter, Vice President of Corporate Affairs, Jostens Learning Corporation.

Glenn H. Crumb, Professor Emeritus, Western Kentucky University, Bowling Green.

Michael Damyanovich, Project Director for Computer/Technology, Osseo Area Schools, Maple Grove, Minnesota.

Martha Deming, Freelance Writer and Editor. Formerly with The Wisconsin Public Television Network.

Thomas DeRose, Director of Media, Western Washington University, Bellingham. Formerly with the Wisconsin Public Television Network.

Kay Gilliland, Director, EQUALS in Computer Technology, University of California, Berkeley.

Carol C. Kuhlthau, Assistant Professor, School of Communication, Information, and Library Studies, Rutgers University, New Brunswick, New Jersey.

Regan McCarthy, Deputy Director, New York Urban Coalition/Center for Educational Leadership.

Charles Mojkowski, President, Technology Applications Associates, Cranston, Rhode Island.

Dennis Newman, Senior Scientist, Bolt Beranek & Newman, Cambridge, Massachusetts. Formerly Research Scientist, Bank Street College.

Stanley Pogrow, Associate Professor of Educational Administration and Foundations, and developer of HOTS project, University of Arizona, Tucson.

Andee Rubin, Division Scientist, Bolt Beranek & Newman, Cambridge, Massachusetts.

Gregory C. Sales, Assistant Professor, Curriculum and Instructional Systems, and Research Coordinator at the Center for the Study of Educational Technology, University of Minnesota, Minneapolis.

Joyce C. Sherman, Library Media Specialist, Brunswick Acres School, South Brunswick, New Jersey.

Sue Sollie, Blue Earth, Minneapolis Apple Classrooms of Tomorrow.

Benjamin H. Thomas, 7th and 8th Grade social studies teacher at the Sidwell Friends School, Washington, D.C.

Roy Unruh, Physics Department, University of Northern Iowa, Cedar Falls.

Gilbert Valdez, Manager, Instructional Design, Minnesota Department of Education, St. Paul.

Cynthia Warger, Educational Consultant at Warger, Eavy and Associates, Reston, Virginia.

Mary Alice White, Professor of Psychology and Director of the Electronic Learning Laboratory, Teachers College, Columbia University, New York.

Frank B. Withrow, Team Leader, Technology Applications Group, Programs for the Improvement of Practice, Office of Education Research and Improvement, United States Department of Education.